GW00857786

Surviving Your Year Abroad
By Nicola Beedle

Amor, nunca podré agradecerte lo que has hecho por mi y por este proyecto. Tuya, eternamente.

Contents

Welcome to Surviving Your Year Abroad: Get Ready and Get Excited!

When the idea for this book popped into my head just before my own year abroad, I dismissed it, thinking that it was "only me" who would be interested in information about how to get the most out of my year abroad and what pitfalls might lay ahead of me. Then in January 2012, roughly 9 months after I graduated from the University of Leeds, I decided to do some research.

The results were astounding! After surveying over 200 ex-year abroad students and then conducting in-depth interviews with over 50 of them, there was a clear signal that yes, it is fantastic to go on your year abroad and take it as an adventure, but almost everybody said that they would have liked to have had more information about going on year abroad from ex-year abroad students. After 7 months of hard work, the result of all those surveys and interviews is before you: a treasure trove of information about going on a year abroad from people who have actually been there and done that.

This book tries to encapsulate all of the information that was given to me by some very generous and kind students from all over the UK. Almost everything and anything about going on a year abroad was spoken about: safety, your first day, week, and month, bureaucracy and, most importantly, getting the most out of your year abroad so that you have an amazing year!

I really wanted to give you all the information possible to make sure you have an amazing year abroad, to show you the ups and downs that you might encounter, and to give you the best tips to make sure that you have a worry-free year abroad.

So, sit back, enjoy and get ready and get excited about your year abroad!

Chapter 1: Before you go

There's a lot to think about before you even get on the plane and start the amazing journey that is your year abroad and I'm here to help you make the best start to your year abroad as possible. There's lots you can do to make your year abroad go easier even before you set foot in the country: from deciding whether or not to arrive early to preparing yourself linguistically.

Planning before you go can make the difference between an easy but tiring day and a hellish, stressful one. With that in mind, let's take a look at some of the tips and tricks that previous year abroad students have mentioned about planning before you go:

Essential Preparations

Get in touch with your contact

Before you leave, it's vital that you get in touch with the in-country contact that you have been given. This could be the English teacher at your school, the International Office at your host university or your superior or predecessor at your work placement. Either way, getting in touch with them is essential. Not only will they be able to guide and help you with your search for accommodation and prep you on what to expect when you arrive but it's quite possible that they will be one of your only contacts once you arrive. Also, if they know when you will arrive, it's possible that they might get in touch and offer to meet you and show you around.

These people can provide insightful advice about the town or city where you will be living for the next year and will be able to help you out with accommodation and those first few days.

I was extremely lucky with my contact. She was lovely and came and met me at the bus station when I arrived from accompanying my mum and sister to the airport. We went for a drink where we chatted away about the school and she told me how lovely the people there were. She showed me around and really helped me feel at home. We then arranged for me to go into the high school where I was teaching before I was due to start so that I could find my way around and introduce myself to the teachers I would be working with. Having a good contact and being friendly and open with them and letting them know how you are getting along is essential on your year abroad. It's the one person you can really get to know and trust to support you when your first few days pass by in a flurry of people, places and new words. On my first day at work, I met lots and lots of people and it was so hard to keep up with all the names, not to mention all the Spanish that was spoken so quickly, but my contact helped me and supported me through the whole day. Your contact is the person that will be there to help you.

If your contact cannot meet you personally, there may be some sort of programme or group you can join where everyone meets up at the airport at a certain time or where a student at your university meets you at the airport and shows you around their university. Here's E. Johnson's (Germany) experience:

"I signed up to a programme that the International Centre ran, which meant that I was met at the airport by a student (who could have spoken English to me, but I chose to speak German) and he then took me back to the University Campus and helped me sort out my room. He left me with instructions of how to get to the food shop, how to set up the internet and how to get to where we were next meeting to go through more formalities. Everything ran smoothly, even though I went a different way to the shops."

These can be really great programmes because you get the benefit of talking to a student or work colleague and meeting people right from the start.

Preparing yourself linguistically

If you're going to a country where your native language is not spoken, preparing yourself linguistically for your year abroad is a must. After the academic teaching year ends, for most people this is in May or June, you have at least two months (sometimes three!) before you go on your year abroad. Not having contact with any language for one month or more can have a negative effect on your language skills. It's essential to make sure you read, write, listen or speak the language of the country you are going to in the months leading up to your year abroad, even if you've finished university for the year.

I know, this is much easier said than done, especially after the stress of exams. But it's a must if you want to feel fully prepared for your year abroad. It's not wise to go from not having spoken the target language for up to three months to being dumped in the deep end, trying to get by. Even just 30 minutes a day of contact can really help you get used to the accents/language variations of the region you are going to. Like me, I had spent my academic career, up until my year abroad, listening to speakers from Madrid and, for the most part, the north of Spain. Then, I turned up in Eastern Andalucía. I suddenly found myself face to face with people speaking with heavy Andalucian accents (i.e. no d's, s's and, occasionally, c's pronounced as s's!). I can tell you something – I understood about 5 words on my entire first day! So, my words of wisdom? Try and listen to the accent of the place where you're heading before you go! You might save yourself a bit of red-faced embarrassment, unlike me.

Here are a few other ideas of small things you can do before you go on your year abroad to prepare you for going:

- If you have the opportunity, speak with natives
- Set up a language exchange with natives
- Practice speaking your target language with people on your course
- Read the national newspaper of your new host country online
- Listen to some podcasts or short videos in the target language
- Watch a movie in the target language
- Listen to the radio (if possible).

Doing just one of these things, once a day, for about half an hour before you go can really help you once you arrive. This way you won't be diving into your year abroad without having spoken the language of the country for nearly 3 months.

Research, research, research

A lot of previous year abroad students spoke about the importance of researching, in-depth, the region, town, university, school, workplace you are going, before you go. As fun as it is to turn up and have an adventure, planning ahead can save you some headaches.

And the research doesn't just stop at researching the area or what you will be doing for the next year, planning such things as bus routes from the airport and what time they stop running etc. can really help you to start your year abroad smoothly.

Planning your trip

Planning your journey to your host country involves a lot of decisions alone, never mind the rest of your year abroad! In this section, you'll find a few tips and hints that previous year abroad students highlighted.

Touch down

Deciding when you are going to arrive is entirely down to you and it all depends on what you are going to do. Here are a couple of things to bear in mind:

- Arriving late on a night is not a good idea, there may be no one around to collect you, there may be no public transport, getting your bearings is much easier during the day too.
- Try to avoid Sunday. Arriving on a Sunday can spell problems if you are travelling to a country which generally winds down on a

> *Real Student Experience*
>
> *"I was lucky as I had a friend who was staying in the same place as me for her year abroad so we travelled out together which made the day less stressful as I wasn't alone! I also knew several other people from Durham who had already arrived in Aix so to some extent they could help prepare us!... On the bus we met another English girl who teamed up with us as she was alone and unsure what to do."*
> *Elizabeth Lewis, France*

Sunday. In some countries, such as Spain, it's still quite customary (unless you're in a tourist area) for most shops, bars and supermarkets to be closed on a Sunday – not good when you're trying to do your first shop. I arrived late on a Saturday night and I woke up on Sunday to find almost everywhere closed – I definitely hadn't reckoned for that! The thing was, I had no food in the house and had to find something for breakfast. I walked around the town for about 20 minutes before I found a bar which was open. I waked in an everyone was eating the same thing... some sort of cake with chocolate sauce. I had no idea what this was nor what it was called, so what did I do? I had to walk up and ask the man behind the bar what everyone was eating. Well, you can imagine how they all looked at me! And needless to say I went bright red! The worst thing was, I didn't even understand his answer to my question! I had no choice but to say "one of those then, please" and sit down at a table. I later found out they were *churros con chocolate* but how embarrassing! So, my words of wisdom here are definitely don't arrive on Sundays and take a bit of food with you!

- Give yourself some time – try to arrive a few days to a week before your placement or course is due to start. Spend that time getting to know your new home and exploring the surroundings. This is the perfect time to meet your new friends too!

Going alone or going with friends

Going alone and going with friends both have advantages and disadvantages to them. Some people like their year abroad to be an adventure right from the very start and so they prefer to travel alone to their destination.

Others prefer to have the comfort of friends and family over the first few days, even though they'll meet their new friends very soon and, as the situation commands, will get to know them very well. Taking friends and family with you (or it being a happy coincidence that they just happen to be going on holiday to the same place you are heading to on your year abroad) can be really helpful. As B. Harker (France) states:

"I went with my parents for the first few days, with them staying in a hotel. It was hard to organise getting my room and I had to go to several offices around the city to get keys sorted so having a stable room in a hotel was nice and it was nice to know if something couldn't be done I would have somewhere to stay." B. Harker, France

It's good to know, too, whether or not people from your home university are going to the same area or university as you. If so, it might be possible to arrange to meet at the airport, be on the same plane or just meet up once you are there. This can prove invaluable if they have been there for a few days longer than you, have already done everything and are able to give you some first-hand advice about what you need to do and when you need to do it.

If no one from your university is going on their year abroad to the same place as you, you never know, you might meet someone on the plane or on the bus or train to where you are going who is in the same situation as you. Be open to the situation and know that the people waiting for you at the other end will be more than happy to help.

Packing

Packing for your year abroad can be stressful. Fitting your life into a suitcase is not easy but it is possible and if you think clearly and plan what your year abroad is really going to be like (by reading this book, for example), you can decide what you need or don't need.

One note before we carry on. Research is essential! I went to the south of Spain and everyone tells you about how hot it will be. But by not researching, I was caught massively by surprise by how cold it got in winter! It was absolutely freezing! And what's worse I didn't know how badly prepared many Spanish homes are for the cold (no central heating etc.) which makes it even worse. I had hardly packed any winter clothes, and I needed serious winter clothes, big thick jumpers which I don't even wear at home in the north of England! Moral of the story – do your homework to avoid being caught out!

Another good idea is to look at the prices of things in the area where you will be (you can take a look at our budget reports – drawn up from information obtained from ex-year abroad students – at www.survivingyouryearabroad.com/budgetreports). That way, if you find that anything is really expensive, you can try and take it with you.

Really, it all depends on where you are going and what you are doing and previous year abroad student experiences ranged from people who took very little with them (and bought the essentials there) and others who took far too much. Everyone took different things and it really depends on what you are like as a person and what you might need on your year abroad.

Here's a boiled down list of things you might need on your year abroad:

- Documents (passport, EHIC or other health insurance details, year abroad insurance details, passport photos etc.)
- Home university information
- Host university information
- If arriving on a night, something to eat once you get in
- An extension cable (so you only need one travel adaptor)
- Any medicines you need and believe you may not be able to find on your year abroad.
- Clothes for the changeable seasons (research is really important here!)
- Little things to remind you of home, maybe photos of your family and friends
- Maps of your home town or city, postcards, books, DVDs (if you are teaching English)
- Some DVDs or books in your mother tongue

So long as you have the first three items on the list above, the rest is up to you. Another good find are vac-pack bags. They're just bags that you can use a hoover to suck the air out so that they are a lot smaller and you can fit more in your bag.

Another money saver is an extension cord. I hadn't thought of this but I wish I had! Packing one extension cord and one travel adapter is so much easier than trying to find travel adapters for all your electrical goods or trying to alternate with just one adapter when you really want to listen to your MP3 player and charge your phone at the same time!

Personally, I took far too much stuff and ended up having to leave a lot when I came back to the UK – remember, you can accumulate a lot in a year!

Chapter 2: Your First Day

Or, in other words, a day of travel, sleeping and speaking those first few words in a foreign language.

Your first day, no matter where you end up in the world, is probably going to be one of the most stressful days of the entire year: emotionally charged and physically tiring. Also, you'll probably have a lot less time than you originally thought, so leaving yourself plenty of time to get things done is an excellent idea.

If you manage to think things through and plan everything out before you go (which is a lot easier than you think – just check out Chapter 1: Before You Go), although you'll be tired and grumpy, you'll cope with everything the world may throw at you.

You are really in control of your first day and a lot of what will happens on that day is down to what you've planned to do and where you're going to go and how much time you've given yourself before university or work placements begin.

That said, a few things are always going to happen on your first day: you will be tired, you will speak your first words in a foreign language (supposing you're going to a non-English speaking country), and you will realise just what a big deal this is.

Tiredness

N. Maximchuk went on a very long flight to Australia and in her own words was "grumpy and tired! When I got back I made something to eat, made my bed and went to sleep for a long time!" I can't put it better myself! Whether you are going far away for your year abroad or whether you only a short trip to cope with, you will be more tired than you think you will be. Firstly, travelling is tiring – as many of you will already know – but what's not to be forgotten is that this is going to be quite an emotional day. You're going to be saying goodbye to friends/family, travelling, dealing with airports, ports and border control and not to mention the realisation that night when you finally stop that you really are doing this and that you have a whole year ahead of you.

Real Student Experience

"My first day was fairly uneventful. I'd already made contact with a tutor (an older student) at the university here. She was very helpful. She met me at the train station and then she took me to my student accommodation. This was very helpful as my accommodation is the other side of town, so if I was on my own I would have found it very overwhelming, especially after the journey. Anna Mathers, Germany

Hola, Bonjour, Hallo

Ah... those first few words. Whether you're nervous, excited or down right dreading it – you will have to speak those first words.

Believe me, the first ones are the worst if you're nervous and then it gets better from there. My first few words were to a bus driver. I had been on a bus for 5 hours from Malaga to my new town in Linares, Jaén. I was tired, done in and worst of all... I had no idea where I was. This bus said it was going to Linares but 5 hours in and I was still seeing nothing but olive trees and small towns. So, this was it! I had to go up to bus driver and find out if this was actually the right bus or whether I had got on the wrong bus. There I was walking up to him, all these Spaniards looking at me, and I asked him when we'd be arriving in Linares.

Much to my relief, he said "in 30 minutes". My broken Spanish had won through and it wasn't as bad as I had built it up to be! My Spanish was far from great but I had coped – and so will you!

The other thing to remember, as Ed Millar, who spent his time abroad in France and Peru, said "You're not going to understand much on your first day." And you really won't. Unless you've been there and spent lots of time speaking the language before, your first day, week... even month... is going to be very difficult as you get to know the accent of your particular area and find your confidence. But don't worry, little by little you'll improve (remember, one of the best ways to improve your speaking is to speak with natives and not hide away with your friends from home – see Chapter 7).

Meeting your new "family"

Your new family could be anyone and everyone! Be open to everyone you meet and you'll have an amazing time. Your new family is going to be your rock further next year. They're the ones who are going to be there when things get rough, they're the ones who going to be there when you feel a bit blue and they're going to share some of the best moments of your life.

Unlike your friends at home, who you tend to choose in life, your friends from your year abroad are people who you will have met through circumstance. In other words, you're all in the same boat together. Through hell and high water, your year abroad friends will help you get through the best and the not so great moments on your year abroad. And trust me meeting them will be a lot easier than you think.

If you're worried that you're not going to meet anybody on your year abroad and you're worried about being alone, stop worrying! Out of everybody who have interviewed about year abroad, nobody has ever had that experience. Okay sometimes you might not get along with some people but you will meet people and together you will have a great time.

There are lots of opportunities to meet your new family and new friends could be anywhere so make sure, right from the very start, that you take every opportunity to meet people and say yes to every opportunity that presents itself.

Even on your very first day there will be ample opportunity to meet and get to know new people. If you've managed to get in touch with somebody who's going to be in the same town as you, why not meet up with them for a drink when you arrive. Of course this might not always be feasible especially if you've been on their nine-hour flight and by the time you get to your destination you're jetlagged and all you want to do is sleep but try make an effort to make sure that you don't miss out on anything.

Your First Full Day

OK, so your first day of your year abroad might be spent travelling and you might feel that your first real day is actually the first full day after you arrive. Most previous year abroad students suggested making the most of that day by getting to know people and getting to know your town.

For example C. Lorbiecki, who spent her year abroad in Mexico, spent her first full day with the other languages assistants and she mentioned that they even organised a trip on her very first day. They decided to visit somewhere together so that they could hang out and get to know each other. This is a really great idea because it gives you the chance to get to know people, get off on the right foot and not miss out on anything. I mean, seriously, who wouldn't want to start your year abroad by seeing something new on your very first day.

Emotions

It's quite possible that travelling to your new home will pass by in a daze of luggage, flights and transfers and it won't hit you that you won't see your friends and family for months until you actually arrive, sit down and breathe.

There's nothing wrong with being upset over leaving. I remember on my first night, I cried. Not because I thought that my year abroad was going to be horrid or anything like that, but because it was such an emotionally charged day, I was shattered from flights and bus transfers and then having to say goodbye to my family was not easy, especially when you're walking away from the familiarity of home and into the unknown world of your new town or city.

This is entirely normal. Don't stress about being a bit emotional on your first day. It's a big upheaval and you'll soon start having far too much fun and there'll be too many new sights to see to stay sad for long.

It's probably going to be the first night when it's really going to hit you that you are abroad and that you are not going to see your family and friends for a while. Most year abroad students have highlighted this is something that they didn't see coming and would have liked to have known about it because it can really catch you off guard.

The best way to deal with this is to remember that you're going to have a great year abroad and that this is just the culmination of all your preparation, all your hard work and a very stressful and tiring day. It's in times like these when it's a really good idea to have some mementos with you, like, photos of your friends and family. These little mementos can really help you out when you're feeling a little bit down. The best bet is to get some sleep and wake up in the morning ready to start your year abroad adventure.

Furnishings, Food and First Days

Finding out whether or not your accommodation comes with bed sheets, kitchen equipment etc. can be difficult and sometimes you won't get an answer until you are actually there.

Several students pointed out that in their experience, they turned up and their halls or their new flat had no supplies like bed sheets or quilts at all. The best thing to do in this situation is to do your upmost before you go to find out what you are going to need. Failing that, if you do turn up and there are no essential items, there are two options. You can go out to a cheap shop near you and buy your essentials or as Anna

Mathers (Germany) did, you can see if you find a student at your university who is leaving or who is moving to a new place and buy their stuff off them.

If you go for option one, ask around and find out where the cheapest place is to get sheets and bedding. Normally the big supermarkets have such things or there are cheap bazaars around where you can find dirt cheap essentials (like I did when I found out I needed quite a few things for the apartment). One of the best people to ask in this case would be your contact at your university or work placement or to ask someone who has already been there and done that – like ex-year abroad students.

Don't let nerves get the better of you

It's normal to be nervous on your first day so try not to let it stress you out. Meeting new people and getting to know a new town can be daunting but if you relax and enjoy yourself, you'll find that you have a much better experience and things will run smoother.

Get to your destination as soon as possible

Real Student Experience:

"The following days were quite stressful looking for somewhere to live, but I made a clear decision on the first day to just go with the flow and worry tomorrow." Ed Millar, France and Peru

Whether you've got a flat waiting for you or if you're planning on spending a few nights in a hostel while you look for accommodation, get to wherever you are staying quickly. You'll be grateful once you can dump your stuff and get on with everything else you have to do.

Always have a plan B

You never know what's going to happen and you can't plan for everything as Ed Millar (France and Peru) found when he landed in Lima. His suitcase hadn't made the connection in Madrid and he was stuck in searing heat wearing long sleeved clothing. On top of that, it would take five days for his suitcase to arrive. So what did he do? "I tried to get over the jetlag and rest". In these kinds of situations, stressing and worrying aren't going to help you out and, in fact, can become your worst enemy. The situation is what it is and if you can, try and relax and enjoy the extra couple of days in the airport or hotel that's presented itself to you as an opportunity.

> *Real Student Experience:*
>
> *"When I arrived in Hamburg, my suitcase didn't arrive with me as it had got mislaid in between flights. This was my first language test! Having a friendly face waiting at arrivals meant that I was able to laugh rather than cry about the first challenge."* Natalie Blackburn, France and Germany

Even if you're getting picked up at the airport by your university or your colleagues at work, always make sure you know exactly where you need to go just in case they don't turn up or a problem arises. Just make sure that you know where to go and what you need to do. Whether you're spending a year abroad at a university or on a work placement or teaching English, you should always find out where you need to go and what you need to do .

Whatever comes your way, you have the means and the resources to tackle it – no matter how big or stressful it seems.

Bureaucracy

The fact is that you will probably have to do some sort of form filling on your first day, especially if you are going to spend your year abroad at university. This can be stressful and can be a bit much, but going with the flow has been the recommendation of most students who have been in the same situation.

Also, bureaucracy can start before you even get into the country – at border control. This isn't some much a problem if you are staying within the EU but if you travelling further afield, bear in mind that border control must be taken seriously. It can be quite stressful, as A. Woods pointed out when he went to the USA "It was very nerve racking. Immigration and customs was a horrendous experience, taking forever and nearly causing me to miss my connecting flight."

There's always a chance that bureaucracy will hold you up so plan ahead and leave yourself extra time if you need to get through border control and immigration.

Get by with a little help from your friends

It really is down to you how you want to start your year abroad. Personally, I chose to have my mum and sister come with me for the first weekend. Not only did it mean I had more baggage weight by using their half-filled suitcases, but it also meant that there was some support for me while I was getting on my feet. They stayed for the weekend and then went home, leaving me to get to know my new family. Of course, other people choose to do it differently and there are people who went alone, others who went with their family for a few weeks and other combination of family/friend trips.

One option I hadn't realised and which might help you if you are studying or working in the same area as one of your friends is to stay at their house for the first night or have them come to your house. This was what Sonia Devi did who went to France:

"The best thing to do on your first day alone is to invite a friend over to stay the night, or go and stay with them. It helps you settle in better and makes you feel a lot better knowing that there's someone there for emotional support and to help you with little day to day issues." Sonia Devi, France

You never know what might happen

Just say yes to whatever comes your way, stay safe, and really enjoy your year abroad from the start.

And don't forget: this is only the beginning!

Chapter 3: Accommodation

Finding somewhere to live while you're on your year abroad can be one of the most stressful things you will do.

There are several options when it comes to your living conditions while you're away: living with natives, other international students or alone, location, price, close to town, close to your school or work place.

Let's start off with a key question: whether to live with natives, other international students or alone. Each option has its benefits and downsides and it's really down to how you would like to live and what you would like to do while you're away. Here, I'll start by looking at the case for living with natives.

Living with natives

Although it will mean you have to speak in the target language all the time (that's one of the main reasons for a year abroad, right?!), it is great for learning a language. Even if your language skills aren't great, living with natives and having to communicate with them every day, even if it's only about who will cook that night, will help you improve your language skills in leaps and bounds.

> *Real Student Experience*
>
> *... [T]he best way to integrate is to live in a flat share with native speakers. Elizabeth Lewis. France*

Not only are there linguistic benefits to consider, living with natives means that you're with someone who knows the area and who knows all about the country. They'll be able to show you the best places to eat, drink, and visit as well as tell you about other 'off-the-beaten-track' sights that you may not have known about otherwise. Hey, you never know, if you become really great friends, you might end up meeting their family and being invited around to their house and spending time with them - and I can tell you this is a real treat and you get to speak so much of the language and get to know them so well that you'll end up meeting up a couple of times over your year abroad.

Real Student Experience:

I wish I had known the real benefits of living with local students! Anon. Madrid

Living with Friends/Non-Natives

It can seem very appealing to live with people either from your home university or people who speak great English but this can also have a negative effect on your year abroad. By living with non-natives, you won't get the benefit of finding out about 'off-the-beaten-track' places, but you may get to know people from other parts of the world, meaning you have somewhere to crash, if you decide to visit their part of the world.

Although this may seem like a great option to you, beware of the disadvantages of living with non-natives. These can include not speaking the local language, not getting to know new places and returning to your home university feeling like you've not taken advantage of the opportunity (this can be even worse if you are on a language course and have been aware for the year and hardly spoken any of the target language).

Halls of residence

When speaking to year abroad students, opinion was really divided over whether or not you should live in the student accommodation provided by your host university. The main problem with choosing to live in halls of residence while you are away is that you are normally placed with other international students or with your fellow English-speaking university friends. Don't get me wrong – there's nothing bad about wanting to spend your year abroad with your friends but in order to make the most out of your year abroad, you really want to live with natives.

There are up sides to halls of residence and student halls such as being with people who are in the same situation as you, you'll get to know people from lots of different countries and your accommodation is sorted for you and you don't have to do a great deal in order to find somewhere to live.

The downsides, apart from not living with natives, is that some students found that they ended up speaking lots of English – with that being the common language amongst international students -, not getting to see as many unknown sights as fellow international students didn't know about them, and that it was pot luck as to whether the student accommodation was good or bad.

When to choose

Everybody does this differently. For me, I really wanted the security of having somewhere as soon as I arrived so I sought out my accommodation online and it was ready for me when I arrived. There are some downsides to this such as not being able to look around before you pay your deposit, having to pay a deposit to hold the flat to someone you don't know (and don't know whether you can trust or not) and not knowing the area very well (although your contact can always help with this). I was really lucky and had a great experience with my landlady but, as you know, you have to be really careful when trying to rent flats or houses over the internet.

If you're looking to rent before you leave your home country, make sure your research is thorough and try and find out as much as possible about your future landlord before you head out (it's possible, if you live in a small town, that your contact might know them).

A lot of other ex-year abroad students mentioned how they booked into a hotel or hostel as soon as they arrived for a few days and then spent the first day or couple of days flat hunting. This is a really great idea and it's much safer to rent your year abroad house this way as you'd be able to get to know your future flatmates, find out what the landlord is like first-hand (not just over email) and you're able to pay the deposit and start living in the flat there and then.

Both ways of going about it has its pros and cons but it can be really fun and exciting to do.

A word about contracts

If you've been living out at university, you'll know all about rental property contracts. Abroad this can be a fuzzy area with some countries having very strict rental conditions and others not even offering you a contract! (Even if they don't offer you a contract, go ahead and request one in writing – it's always a good idea to cover your back). Check the terms of your lease and make sure you're not tied into a year if you're only going to be in the country for nine months. Also make sure you understand exactly what the contract says, if it's in a foreign language and you don't fully understand, ask your contact or someone you know and trust over there to have a read and explain the fine details to you.

Also, don't be afraid to ask for things to be changed! If the contract states 9 months but you'll only be there for 6 – don't just throw the towel down, ask your landlord or landlady to see if it's possible to change this. More often than not, they'll be more than happy to change the conditions so that they have a new tent.

If you're renting from someone who is not the owner, for example, if your flatmate has the original contract and then you sub-let a room from them, make sure the details are fully fleshed out as to what part of the bills each flatmate has to pay along with cleaning schedules and other minor details. This may seem tedious but it can stop you, or your flatmate, feeling like you're paying for everything, or paying more than you should be, when this can be resolved before hand.

Check out the payment details too. Again, these vary wildly depending on the country but some will want cash in hand (would they come to the flat or would be expected to drop in on them every month like I had to?) while others prefer a transfer directly into their bank account (so, you'd need to set up a bank account or a transfer from your UK account – watch out for charges though!).

These are some of the ways ex-year abroad students found their accommodation:

- EasyPiso.com

- ESN.org (Erasmus Student Network – funded by the European Commission)
- Padmapper (for apartments in Montreal)
- Rental agencies
- Family connections
- Your contact
- jobwohnen.at (for Austria)
- Gumtree.com
- www.appartager.fr (for France, especially flat sharing)
- Host university student union website
- Loquo.com
- Asking the previous year abroad student at your school or work placement
- www.rentfaster.ca and www.calgary.kijiji.ca (for Canada)
- Ask if anyone someone at your home university whether they know anyone who is or may be renting their property
- Wg-geuscht.de (for Germany and Austria)
- www.studentenwerk-hannover.de (for Hanover)
- www.easywg.at (for Austria)

If you've noticed the distinct lack of US places on the list above, that's because most ex-year abroad students I spoke to had to go into on-campus student accommodation but got to pick and choose their rooms and halls. If you're heading to the US, this is probably what will happen for you and you'll get more information from your host university as and when application deadlines come along.

Chapter 4: Money

Money is a worry for many students throughout the world and this is highlighted for year abroad students who are abroad alone, normally, for the first time and have to manage their money (to be able to afford the flight home, for example).

Money, although it will not make you happy, can cause a lot of stress when things aren't going so well. My aim here is to calm your worries and point you in the direction of help, should you ever need it, and point out some financial help which, regardless of your situation, will bring down the cost of your year abroad.

When I was surveying and interviewing ex-year abroad students one comment really stood out to me *"I wish I had known about financial planning."* That exact quote was taken from an anonymous contributor who spent time in Spain and Germany, but the same feeling was echoed throughout the initial surveys with year abroad students.

Something had to be done about this and what better way than to dedicate an article to it, so that everyone gets the chance to have the knowledge that has been passed on from ex-year abroad students regarding this. So, let's start at the very beginning.

Before You Go: Tell your bank!

You may be thinking that I've gone a bit mad but this can save you a lot of worry and stress throughout your year abroad. By telling you bank that you will be away for a year, they'll be able to make sure that anti-fraud systems are cancelled (so your card doesn't get blocked while away) and they'll be able to set up other features that might be useful to you. With this in mind, here's a three step guide to preparing your bank account:

a. Set up online banking (if you don't have it already) – this will allow you to see what exactly is going on with your account while you're away. This may seem pretty straight forward but if you don't have online banking, you'll be reduced to having to ring up to get your balance (important for budgeting) and to check that no unusual transactions have taken place (fraud prevention!). PS: Remember to always log in using a secure connection so that your details are protected.

b. Tell your bank that you are going away – different banks have different ways of doing this; some let you do it online, others want you to ring up their call centre and with others you have to go into branch. This can seem like a waste of time or a big hassle but, again, it saves a lot of heartbreak and worry along the line! Imagine you go on a night out or need some money quickly for your deposit on your flat but surprise, surprise, your bank has blocked your debit card because you didn't tell them you were away and they think a fraudster is using your card – they do this to protect you and your money but it's just easier all round to tell them before you go.

c. Set up someone you trust as a named and authorised person on your account – not many people know that this is possible but you can authorise someone on your bank account so that if anything goes wrong and you can't get to the branch or call the call centre (because it would cost you more than what's in your bank), the other person can go into branch or call up and everything will be sorted out much quicker and easier. Imagine you lose your bank card, at home you would just ring up and cancel it and get them to send you a new one. However, you're away in France and don't really fancy the massive telephone bill for calling a call centre from abroad; if you have authorised someone on your bank account, they can call up, cancel your card and request a new one – sounds much easier, doesn't it? WARNING – this must be someone you know and trust explicitly, possibly a very, very close family member or friend as they have access to your bank details and we wouldn't those going astray now, would we?

Just those three simple steps will save you a lot of heartbreak, worry and stress during your time abroad.

Before You Go: Saving and Deals

Saving Before You Leave

A lot of ex-year abroad students highlighted how they didn't realise how expensive their year abroad was going to be, and a lot of the advice pointed to saving before you go - you may think you'll be able to scrimp and save during your year abroad, but when you've moved to another country, you are going to want to be going out and socialising.

There are a couple of ways you can save for your year abroad. The most obvious one is to save while you are in your first two years of university. However, students have highlighted that they also got secondary, part-time jobs while they were away (subject to visa and grant restrictions) while others asked friends and family to donate to a year abroad fund instead of buying them birthday and Christmas presents. Another way is to make sure you are given any money you are entitled to such as Maintenance Grants and there are also Maintenance Loans available if you feel that that is a good idea for you.

So how much will I need?

Well, this depends entirely on what you will be doing, whether you will be earning any money and where you are going (as some places are more expensive than others). Try and plan to have at least enough money to cover your basic day-to-day expenses plus prices for flights and travelling. Here at Surviving Your Year Abroad, I've put together some budget reports containing information that ex-year abroad students have given me. You can get your free copy by signing up to the Surviving Your Year Abroad Newsletter at www.survivingyouryearabroad.com. The best option here is to save as much as possible so that you can really enjoy your year abroad.

Note: Ex-year abroad students who travelled to Sweden, Norway and Australia especially commented on how expensive living there was and how they had not prepared sufficiently for this - check out the Budget Reports for more information.

Travel Reimbursements

Many year abroad students are not aware of the fact that they can be reimbursed for travel costs to their year abroad destination, so long as you will be staying there for more than 6 months. Check out the Student Finance England's website for more information here: http://www.direct.gov.uk/prod_consum_dg/groups/dg_digitala

ssets/@dg/@en/documents/digitalasset/dg 195933.pdf. Check with your student finance company to find out if you are entitled.

Save Money on the Trip

Before you leave, it's a good idea to shop around for things that you might need - especially flights. Flights can be very expensive and even though you may be entitled to reimbursement, you are the one who has to pay the money out in the first place. Check out comparison websites, www.skyscanner.net and this budget flight checker courtesy of Martin Lewis' website: http://flightchecker.moneysavingexpert.com/

Budgeting

Budgeting can be made very simple. It can be as simple as whipping up an Excel workbook, listing your expenses and columns filled with how much you plan to spend each month on that item.

Now, sticking to your budget is another thing all together and is one of those "easier-said-than-done" things in life. However, if you know how much money you will have and you budget to stay with in it, try not to go outside of it. If you abandon your budget at the start of the year, it can be really difficult to get back into it and you might find yourself playing catch up all year.

Also remember that any grants may not be paid on time. ERASMUS grants tend to be paid quite late so don't depend on this money to see you through your first couple of months and ensure this becomes part of your budget.

Saving Money Abroad

Accommodation

Check to see whether there are any money-off deals you can take advantage of on your accommodation. For example, in France, many ex-year abroad students mentioned that the CAF, although a long winded task, can save you a lot of money off your rent. This is a financial aid that is offered by the government to students to help them pay their rent. It is complicated to apply for because French bureaucracy can be pretty exhausting/precise but it's worth it in the long run as you receive a generous sum of money. La CAF (caisse d'aide familiale) is the office which deals with family benefits, student finance etc. It's website can be found here: http://bit.ly/hvmr38

For step by step instructions on how to apply for CAF, visit www.survivingyouryearabroad.com/caf-step-by-step.

Travelling

Travelling is going to be one of the most important parts of your year abroad. You are going to see and experience things that you never would have been able to as a tourist. Your native co-workers or student friends will be able to tell you the best places to go and, sometimes more importantly, the places to avoid. However, travelling can be expensive. Here are a few tips on how to keep your travelling costs down:

- Book in advance to save money on train fares and flights
- If there is a group of you going, go for a group booking to save money on flights
- STA travel have some good deals for students on flights and experiences

- Check out rail cards in your country as many offer substantial discounts if you are going to be travelling a lot.
- Try and keep food costs down while travelling by preparing yourselves packed lunches and make a picnic in the first part you find on arrival.
- Go where the natives go to make sure you are not ripped off in tourist hot spots.
- Check out the travel sections of the Surviving Your Year Abroad Budget Reports, free when you sign up for the newsletter, as these contain country-specific advice on the best ways to save money while travelling.
- The Surviving Your Year Abroad newsletter keeps you up to date with fresh tips and ideas (sign up here: www.survivingyouryearabroad.com).

Unforeseen Costs

There can be several unforeseen costs on your year abroad. These can be anything from having to travel home for some unknown reason, having to take a week off work due to illness (let's hope not), or it could be something in the country which you had not planned for. The most pertinent example of this which I came across was a student explaining to me that in Canada the price on the shelf in a shop is not the price you pay at the till (sale tax is added at the till) and in France you may be asked to pay a taxe d'habitation. You can plan for these in your budget and make sure you don't get caught out.

Budgeting for your year abroad is not the most exciting thing in the world, but if you plan correctly and stick to your plan, you can save yourself a lot of headaches in the long-run. Your year abroad will be an amazing time and if you plan correctly, you really can enjoy it all.

Chapter 5: Documents

Documents, documents and more documents: the barrage of documents and forms and bureaucracy both before your year abroad and during the first few weeks can seem never ending. Dealing with this side of a year abroad can be, at times, frustrating and tiresome but there are things you can do before you leave to ease your experience and make the process quicker.

Be prepared

Before you leave, make sure you have all the necessary documents. Make sure you have multiple copies of your passport, birth certificate, driver's license and health insurance card. You'll be amazed how many times you'll be asked to produce a copy and if you do it before you go, you don't have to risk losing important documents when you hand them over to be photocopied. Also, take lots of passport-sized photographs of yourself (at least 8) as you never know when you might need them – student cards, registration,

> *Real Student Experience*
>
> *Germany loves documents/paper work. Check what you need to fill out prior to your departure. Otherwise you might struggle for time once you get there. Anon. Germany*

social security, CAF (if you're going to France), all require these kinds of documents and if you have them ready, the process will be simpler and easier for you.

Get it done

Don't waste time thinking that you'll be able to do it next week or that it won't harm to do it in a month's time – bureaucracy takes a long time no matter where you are in the world – although, it has to be said, some places take a lot longer than others. Dive right in and get it done especially given that in some places there are deadlines which you must adhere to. For example, when going on year abroad to Spain, I had to register with the authorities within three months of arrival. Rather than waiting until the day before the deadline, get it done early and then you don't have to worry while everyone else is running around like headless chickens!

Ask for help

If you get stuck with anything, especially if you are trying to register and fill in forms in a foreign language, ask for help. No one will think any less of you and it is much better to know what you are getting into when signing forms and signing up for bank accounts etc.

Setting Up Your Bank Account Abroad

The idea of going into a bank abroad and setting up your bank account can seem quite daunting, however, as with most things; the worst of it is in your mind. Bankers, despite what the media lead us to believe, are human beings just like you and me and will be really happy to help you set up your bank account for your stay abroad.

As always, your contact at your host university, school or work place should always be your first point of call. They'll know what you will have to do to get a bank account, they may know of fee-free bank accounts and they might even be able to accompany you and lend you a helping hand at understanding what it is you're signing up to.

When I interviewed ex-year abroad students, I found that everyone's experience had been really positive in this regard. Here's what they had to say about setting up their bank accounts:

Germany

"The process for getting a bank account was fairly easy, but my tutor helped me with that. It only took about 10 minutes or so. I had to go to the main branch of my chosen bank in town. I think I had to fill out a form, with important data such as my address in Würzburg, name, date of birth the usual stuff. I think I then had to put about 90 euros in to open it or something along those lines." Anna Mathers

"I needed this Meldezettel (or registration document) in order to get a bank account. I chose Erste Bank as you could get a student account and it was free and there were branches all over the city. I had to wait until I could present my student pass from Vienna university, but it was worth doing this way as I then had an international student identification which you can use anywhere abroad." Jyoti Careswell

France

"Getting a bank account is relatively simple. You need to go to the bank with your passport, a photocopy of your passport, all insurance documents that you have as well as an 'attestation du logement'. Une attestation du lodgement is a document that is either available at the reception of the halls of residence or from your landlord (the rental contract would probably be sufficient) which states that you are officially living there. Some banks charge if you want to open an account for less than year but it is usually about 4 euros per month and it is worthwhile keeping your bank account for longer if you plan to stay in the country for the summer. Once at the bank with all these documents it is just a case of having a chat with one of the assistants and explaining what you want/your situation. On the whole they are usually very nice and helpful and will explain anything you don't understand!" Elizabeth Lewis

"You'll need to make an appointment to see someone within the branch, and take along things like your passport, and proof of address in France, but that's all. Jennifer Ball

Canada

"Bank accounts were pretty easy to set up, once you have an address and telephone number. I would suggest getting a Canadian sim card on monthly contract (either at Fido or Rogers) before setting up a bank account so you have a telephone number they can reach you at. Be aware that you are unlikely to be able to buy anything online, unless you have a credit card, which I thought was quite surprising as you can buy things online with a debit card in the UK." Y. Arai

Austria

"Quite relaxed. I registered for a student account at Erste Bank and they didn't seem too fussed by the fact that I wasn't yet an Austrian student. It's worth doing this as well if you're here long-term, as getting money from an English card can be expensive." Bridget Wynne Wilson

Spain

"You have to get a NIE number and then take this to a bank. My advice would be to take someone with you, ideally a Spanish speaker so that you have some help in understanding what you are signing up for!" L. Meaden

Russia

We were recommended not to get bank accounts because the system in Russia can be quite dodgy. For money, I got paid for my job in cash which covered most of my living expenses, and I used my British bank account card there every now and again, and the charges weren't bad at all. Some banks charge a percentage of what you draw out, some a flat fee however much you get out. I tried not to use my card too much, but it was fine when I did." Esther Harper, Russia

Visas

USA

"Visa was easy, quick trip to London (can take a while I'm told). Make sure you check and double check you have done everything required for it beforehand, I almost turned up without one part." A. Potter

"After you get your official offer letter, you fill out a form online (quite long!) and book an appointment at the American Embassy in London. Do this as soon as possible- and to book the appointment ring at a quiet time as you have to pay to ring them! At the Embassy, you have a short interview at the desk and they issue your visa. Be aware you have to pay £15 for courier costs as they keep your passport to check it then send it back to you." M. Nichols, USA

"You have to ring the embassy and go into London, which can be a pricey little trip. This day is as dull as anything, so take a book, or a friend. You also can't take phones in so plan ahead for this. I had a bit of a nightmare with my visa appointment as the person on the phone got my email address spelling wrong and I ended up having to ring back the next day, in a blind panic, and explain that I hadn't received any details. Thankfully they're quite nice, and I think they're used to dealing with students at particular times of the year." J. Higham, USA

Mexico (D.F.)

Go to the Immigration Office in Polanco and get your forms; around the corner there are several offices which promote filling out your forms for you and taking your pictures – you pay them 50-60 pesos (£2.50-£3) and they jump through the hoops for you. This is so much easier than trying to do it yourself. You hand these in and go back in a few weeks to pick up your immigrant card. You will always have to wait a couple of hours in the Immigration Office. C. Lorbiecki

Singapore

Visa stuff is a little bit of a nightmare as you need a Student Pass which you must obtain from the ICA (Immigration and Checkpoints Authority) when you arrive, along with all the correct documentation and it can take two hours. They often make you come back a few days later to collect, but if you request it you can get it on the same day (I did). You'll need lots of passport-sized photos and photocopies of passport too, plus a letter from NUS and another one you get when you apply for the Student Pass online (I think)." O. Reynolds, Singapore

Other Documents

Apart from setting up a bank account, you might also be required to get other documents, such as, a registration card from the local police station or a student card. Here's what ex-year abroad student said about the area you're going to:

Würzburg, Germany

"I also had to register as a citizen of Würzburg, you go to the town hall (Rathaus) for that. I also had to go along to AOK the insurance company, and all they did was scanned my EHIC card. For the first few weeks I had to have a bus pass as well, which again my tutor helped to organise. I had to just fill out a form and of course a passport photo. I came out in September though for an Intensive Language Course. So I needed a bus pass for a month until I got my student ID card. Once you have a student ID card, you can use that for the bus." Anna Mathers

Germany

"I had to register in the city, and get specific insurance for the university student card. It's also worthwhile considering a student travel pass." E. Johnson

Hamburg, Germany

"In Hamburg I had to register with the police. I did this once I received a contract for my flat, and I just had to go to the local office and sign a couple of forms." Natalie Blackburn

Vienna, Austria

"I enrolled at the university (you have to do so online before August 31st and in person by the end of September, and bring all A-Level original certificates along) in order to get an "official" Studentausweis. I needed to "anmelden" at the beginning declaring where I was living, and officially at the "Meldeamt" to declare my "long-term" residence in Austria. This was longwinded but otherwise I think you get fined if you don't do it and the authorities find out." Bridget Wynne Wilson

"I just got a Meldezettel in Austria (like a registration of your address) this involved taking my passport and a signed form from my landlady to a local area office." Jyoti Careswell

France

"Bizarrely in France you have to have 'Third Party Insurance' to go to university in case you break a piece of their equipment. My university supplied me with the necessary insurance but otherwise it is very easy to sort out and there are several stands around which sell this insurance during the 'sign up' period for courses and modules." Elizabeth Lewis, France

"The taxe d'habitation in France: if you rent an apartment privately (not in university accommodation), it's a tax similar to council tax, except students are not exempt. The amount varies and it depends on where the residence is and the square footage." Jennifer Ball

"For finding an apartment I needed details of my parents' income; they had asked for references and previous addresses, but obviously I hadn't lived in France before so I didn't have the papers they would normally require." Jennifer Ball

"I applied for the CAF and they require masses of information, including a full birth certificate, copy of your passport, copy of you EHIC card, bank details and even a written declaration saying that you can pay for your accommodation, plus more." P. Howard

Sweden

"I downloaded the form [for the Swiss identity card] off the Swedish migration website and then went to the migration office in Gothenburg (svingeln) to hand it in and check it was OK." Richard Latham

Russia

[In regards to an immigration card] When you travel into Russia you have to fill out a card (which looks like a really small insignificant piece of paper, but is actually really important!) and give it to the officers at passport control, who keep one half and give you the other half back. You need this when you register your visa (which you have to do within 3 working days of arriving into Russia or going to a new city), and without it you are apparently illegal (because it proves you came into the country through a valid route!)... When we were travelling each of the hostels we stayed in registered our visas for us, so you need it. Esther Harper

Belgium

After registering with the university I had to go to city hall to register. I was then visited by the police after which I was considered resident. Kate Allen

Always remember that if you need any additional documentation, your host university, work placement or school should let you know. If in doubt, always ask.

From all that great advice offered from ex-year abroad students, the most important part to take away is that if you are organised, have your documents ready and ask for help if you don't understand something, the process is quite simple – just take a good book with you in case it takes a while!

Chapter 6: Socializing

Socializing is going to be a big part of your year abroad, whatever you do, and I imagine it's the part you are most looking forward to.

Now, you might be surprised by this but on your year abroad there is a right and a wrong way to socialise.

The wrong way is only socialising with your home friends and not getting out and meeting the locals. The wrong way is to not achieve as much linguistically because you didn't make the effort to really push yourself out of your comfort zone. The wrong way is to really throw away your year abroad because you missed out on all those amazing unknown sights that only locals can tell you about.

(See, there is a wrong way!)

The right way, of course, is to make sure that you get out and meet people, local people and say yes to every opportunity. That's what we're going to take a look at in this chapter: how you can socialise the right way throughout your year abroad.

Meet the natives

The number one thing you can do to make sure you socialise the right way and really make the most of your year abroad is to meet the natives. Yes, this means you will have to push yourself out of your comfort zone. But, this also means you're going to make amazing friends and really benefit linguistically and because who better to show you around a country than the natives?

It's really easy to fall into a routine of meeting up with people from home or other international students (where the common language is probably going to be your native language) rather than mixing with the locals and talking to them. It can be as simple as making sure you participate in class or when someone invites you to a party, say yes. Go up to people and start talking about something you have in common (they're not going to be testing you on the pluperfect tense!).

> Real Student Experience
>
> As a foreigner, people are interested to meet you and ask questions – you have to be open and friendly and this helps makes friends too." A. Woods, USA

Embrace their culture

If you want someone to show you the best of their country, the best thing is to embrace it with open arms. Do you want to try paella? Yes! Do you want to head out for the weekend on a hiking trip to the mountains? Yes! Do you want to meet up with them for a family and friends gathering? Of course you do! By embracing their way of life and their culture, they're more likely to let you in and, also, in turn embrace your culture.

Share your culture, too

So, don't forget to share some of your culture too. Why not invite your new found native friends round for lunch or for an evening meal and cook them some dishes from your native country? Those are bound to go down a treat.

Also, it's normal for people to have lots and lots of questions about you, your home country and your life generally. Be open and honest. It's a great conversation starter and will really help you make new friends.

Make Socialising Educational!

The best way to get the most out of socialising in a linguistic way is to make it educational! Now, don't go turning to the next chapter – bear with me a second!

Now, I'm not talking about getting your grammar books out and testing one another on subjunctives. What I mean is, organise a language exchange or tandem where you partner up with a native speaker of your target language. You then meet up in a café or somewhere a bit quieter and spend about an hour speaking, first in one language and then in another.

This is a great way of learning the language and these exchanges can really blossom into a great friendship. The best way to get these is through word of mouth – maybe your contact at your work placement knows someone who wants to practice or a friend of a friend knows someone. The other way to get them is to look out for posters around the university or put some up yourself. You'll find that there are lots of people eager to practice their speaking skills.

Say yes!

A great way to socialise and get to know the natives is to simply say "yes" to every offer made to you. You'll get to see so many more things and enjoy so many more experiences just by saying "yes" rather than "no" or "I'll think about it". Say

> Real Student Experience
>
> Accept every single invitation. Bridget Wynne Wilson, Austria

"yes" and then see what happens. If you don't like the experience, you can always say "no" next time.

Confidence is key!

Another important aspect about socialising successfully on your year abroad is being confident.

I realise that this is easier said than done and for some people feeling and acting confident does not come easily and can be a real struggle. But even if you're not the confident type, you can be friendly and smile and just generally be approachable which always works best when trying to meet people and have fun.

> *Real Student Experience*
>
> *At the start, be confident and sociable and it will definitely pay dividends (true for most aspects of life when starting afresh). O. Reynolds. Singapore*

Get involved!

Getting involved really is the best way to meet people, whether they're natives or other international students. There are lots and lots of ways to get involved too. Here are a few ideas past year abroad students gave:

- Join clubs
- Do all kinds of activities
- Go to Erasmus/international events
- Join societies
- Join teams
- Take dance classes (I can personally recommend this one!)

- Volunteer
- Teach
- Language exchanges/tandems
- Take up a hobby
- Join a choir or singing group
- Get involved in local events (listen to the radio and read the local paper to find out when they're happening)

See, there are lots of activities you can get involved in and I'm sure you'll be able to add to this list with your own ideas.

Start Before You Arrive!

Yes, you read that right – it is possible to start making friends and socialising before you even arrive at your new home for the next year.

These days with social networking and email at the touch of a button, it's so easy to get in touch with people in a similar situation to you. The best ways to do this is to search on the likes of Facebook and Twitter and all the other social networks for groups of people heading to the same area or university. You'll be able to get acquainted and maybe even organise to meet up before you even get there. There's also the Erasmus Student Network for those of you going on an Erasmus year abroad. They have a great forum you can dive into and try and find someone heading to the same place as you.

Also, check out the Surviving Your Year Abroad Facebook page and post on there – I'm sure you'll find someone on there who is heading to the same place as you. The important thing to remember is that if you don't look, you won't find. Have a look around and email a few people.
The most important thing to remember on your year abroad is that everyone makes friends!

It really is that simple. You will make friends on your year abroad and you will have an amazing time. Be open and enjoy yourself!

Chapter 7: Languages

Depending on what kind of year abroad you are going on, languages either will or won't be a part of your year abroad. If languages are an important part of your year abroad, hold onto your seats because we're going to go through the main things you need to do to get the most out of speaking and learning foreign languages in a different country – and don't worry, speaking isn't half as scary as you think it's going to be – honest!

Before You Go – Brush Up

Don't be afraid of going to town with this one – you can never be fully prepared for those first few words in a new language but you can give it a good go! By brushing up before you go, you'll not only prepare yourself fully for your year abroad but it'll also help to ease those nerves you have around speaking in a foreign language all the time.

One thing to not do (though it is tempting!) is to finish your second year exams in May or June before you go and then not speak another word in your foreign language until August/September time. These 3-4 months of no contact with the language will leave you feeling unprepared and will weaken your abilities to really

> *Real Student Experience*
>
> *Really brush up on listening to native speakers speaking at full speed, as professors don't stop talking for 2 hours. Anon. France*

speak properly and pick up on everything you hear – something you will have to do from the very first second of your year abroad.

Have no fear though, it can be quite easy to maintain contact with the language, it can be as simple as watching a DVD in your target language. You could meet up with an international student at your university who speaks the language of your host country and meet up or email occasionally over the summer. Why not watch the news online or read one of the many newspapers now published online in your target language? You could even subscribe to a podcast or radio show in your chosen language. There are ample opportunities to prepare yourself linguistically, if you decide to take them.

A small note on accents: you may not realise this (or maybe you do, you little boffins!) but most of your lecturers will try and keep their accent quite neutral when speaking in lectures. This is normal and it's to help you understand all the deep complexities of grammar. Unfortunately, this doesn't exactly help you when preparing for your year abroad. Every region has its own accent, no matter how slight and you have to get used to them. You can start to do this before you leave by, once you've found out where you'll be heading on your year abroad, search for local news channels and listen to the news or local programmes where the presenters have the freedom to use their regional accents. You may think this isn't very important, but there are some parts of the world (like Andalusia where I went on my year abroad) where accents can be very different and can really impede understanding. Letters being pronounced like other letters and half of words being "eaten" (as the lovely people from Andalusia called it) when spoken, was extremely confusing and I wish I had known about this before I left, as I would have been more prepared. The good thing is that after a few months, I came to know when parts of words were being missed off and when certain letters should be other letters. You will get used to it! But a little bit of preparation never did anyone any harm.

Dive in

This has to be one of the most exciting and scary parts of your year abroad. You've done all your preparation, you've studied your language for 2 years and now's crunch time: it's time to speak those first couple of words!

I can hear you screaming right now.

But don't fear. Everything will be fine and no one will bite your head off for getting it wrong (which you will - everybody does). There are lots of things you can do to improve your language skills while you're on your year abroad but the most important one: dive in! Get your hand mucky and get stuck in with the locals. Just getting on with it and not worrying about speaking the language will help you progress much further than preferring to say nothing at all because you don't want to get anything wrong. We learn from mistakes. Mistakes are not a bad thing, just a learning curve.

If you feel nervous about speaking in your target language, remember that you are not there to be tested. People in your host country are not there to test you, they are not there to make a list of all the good points and bad points of your speaking skills, they may correct you (it's good to ask them to do this) and this is helpful but they won't be marking you or examining you. Remember that and you won't feel as nervous about speaking in a foreign language.

Get Involved

So once you've jumped in and spoken those first few words in your target language, what more can you do to help improve your language skills? Here are 5 small things you can do every day on your year abroad which will improve your language skills along the way:

1. Get involved with the natives

It's easy to stick to the people you know and it's comforting to speak your mother tongue with the other people from your home university, but this will not improve your language and you could end up kicking yourself at the end of the year that you have not improved as much as you thought you would! It might be easier than you think to get involved with the natives: speak to the native students on your course, ask their advice about the best places to go (you never know, they might offer to take you with their friends), join up to a club or group at university, talk to your colleagues at work and take an interest in their plans, offer to help out at a charity – the list goes on and on. So long as you still live enough

> *Real Student Experience*
>
> *Spend as much time with natives as possible! It is easy to stick with the ERASMUS group (and I did), but my language skills improved a lot more in 2 months working as an au pair over the summer than they did as an ERASMUS with other Leeds students. If you can find a placement/university where there isn't a large group of students from Leeds, this pushes you out of your comfort zone and forces you to make more of an effort. Natalie Blackburn. France and Germany*

time to get your work/studying done, there's no reason why you can't take part in lots of activities with local people which could benefit everyone involved.

2. Organise a language exchange/tandem

   It may be old fashioned but it's true, *the* best way to learn a foreign language is speaking it with an actual person. All the modern technology in the world cannot (yet) replace the immense language learning benefits of sitting face to face with someone and speaking. If you've not got direct access to native people and find it hard to just walk up and say hi to someone, put up leaflets for language tandems or exchanges or speak to natives you already know and find out if they know anyone who would like to take part. For those of you who don't know, a language tandem is where two people sit down to speak for, for example, an hour. They then speak for the first half an hour in person A's native language and then the second half an hour in person B's native language.

3. Make an effort!

   Making an effort goes a long way and that can sometimes be easy to forget. By stepping out of your comfort zone and going up to some and saying hi or offering to help someone with their language skills in exchange for their help with your language skills can really make a different when trying to learn a language. The language won't come to you on its own, you have to make the effort and immerse yourself in it to explore the full potential of your language abilities

4. Stick to You Guns

This can be hard, especially when it is oh so tempting to speak your native language with people you know will be able to understand you but resist temptation. This really will set the tone for your whole year because once you start speaking to them in your native language, it can be so, so difficult to get them to speak to you in their native language. In fact, you really have to be quite insistent in this respect because there will be some people who, although you speak to them in their native language, will be determined to speak to you in your native language. Stick to your guns and you'll improve much more because of it.

5. Enjoy the Results

After all your efforts, make sure you enjoy the amazing results you'll have! It's so easy to get caught up in year abroad travelling and enjoyment that you don't realise what a huge improvement you've made with your language. One of the best ways to keep track of this is to keep a diary in the target

> *Real Student Experience*
>
> *Put yourself out of your comfort zone to improve your language – it's really scary to start but the results are amazing! Esther Harper. Russia*

language and after you've been there for a few months, go back and see all the mistakes you made at the beginning and how you've been improving over your time spent there.

You see, it really can be as easy as following those five steps. Following those five steps might take a bit of effort on your part and it will probably involve you having to push yourself out of your comfort zone but the rewards are worth it in the end!

When You're Back – Keep Practicing

Just a small note to say that you need to remember that you may come home from your year abroad in May/June but you may not go back to university until September. So make sure you keep in touch with those lifelong friends and keep speaking the language!

Chapter 8: The Low Down on Studying

After having chosen to study at university on your year abroad, you're probably wondering what comes next. Well, that's what this chapter is about. When thinking about studying abroad, there are probably two studying-specific questions that are in your mind: how to make the most of it and what will it really be like?

Making sure that you have a great time studying abroad and really get the most out of it is really down to two things: what you do before you go and the second part is what you do when you are there.

Before you head out to your host university there are plenty of things you can do to make sure that your study abroad year gets off to the best possible start.

1. Get in touch with you host university

The very first thing you should as soon as you are accepted onto a study abroad course is get in touch with your host university. They'll provide you with lots of information about accommodation, getting there, the modules and the international student community at that university.

2. Read EVERYTHING you get from your host university and your home university

So, when your host university send you all this information, make sure you read it all. It's easy to brush it aside and keep putting it off because, you know, your year abroad is ages away. It will creep up on you and be here sooner than you think and you don't want to end up being the last one to find out that you should have got in touch with them 6 weeks ago to confirm your accommodation or to have first pick at modules.

On the same lines, make sure you read everything your home university gives you. It may look like just a bunch of paper with common sense information on it, but hidden in there will be some really important pieces of information that you will need going forward like, for example, application deadlines and advice on where to go and what your course requirements are.

3. Ask at your home university (before you go) about modules and credit systems

Many previous year abroad student explained that they had not realised how different the university systems abroad could be and how this could make choosing modules that would fit correctly into their degree really confusing. Get information from your home university about how many credits you need from your host university, how many modules you should take and how the marks will translate across. The study abroad coordinator at your

Real Student Experience

The credit point system is different to the British system so I was very confused about how many modules I had to take in order to pass the year. Anon. Germany

university or in your department should know this information or at least be able to point you in the right direction.

4. Ask your host university about any doubts you have

If the information you want about a certain aspect of your study abroad year is not in the information given to you by either your host or home university, ask them. It's always better to resolve your issues and questions before you go than waiting until you get there and panicking. Keep in mind that study abroad coordinators are usually very busy, both here and abroad, so it may take them a few days to get round to answering your email so it's always a good idea to get in touch with them sooner rather than later.

5. Get in touch with other students at your host university

Social media knows no bounds and almost everybody uses some kind of social media and year abroad students are no different. Check out all the social media platforms to see if there is an ERASMUS or international group at your host university. Nine times out of ten there is one and it can be a really great source of year abroad information and you might even get to know some other international students heading out to your host university before you even leave. This can be a great way to arrange doing the initial 'scary' stuff (paperwork, arriving, finding accommodation etc.) with someone else who is in exactly the same situation as you.

6. Arrive early

I know we covered this in the Before You Go chapter but it's worth repeating: arrive early. Arriving early can make a lot of difference when having to deal with paperwork. It's not as simple as going to see the International Office and getting everything you need there and then. There's a lot of paperwork, you have to find and choose your modules, organise a time table and you don't want to miss out on the best modules for you by arriving late. Leave plenty of time to get all this done before the academic year begins. It can be the difference between starting off on the right or wrong foot.

So now you've done all that and you've finally arrived at your host university, what can you do to make sure you get the most out of your year abroad? "Plenty" is the simple answer to that. All the previous chapters gave you lots of ideas about how to have a fantastic year abroad, either linguistically, through socialising, even down to who you decide to live with, and all those can, and should, be used by you guys going on study abroad. A couple of study-specific things that you could do to enhance your year abroad include joining clubs and societies with other native students, revising for exams and doing project work with other native students that way you can practice the language and find out if you missed something important during a lecture and even putting up leaflets for a tandem language exchange where you and a native student meet up and practice the language between you. There are plenty of things you can do to make your study abroad year amazing, just look for the opportunities and say yes to them.

Now, this is probably the section you've been most interested in from the start of the chapter, finding out what it will really be like. Going to university in another country is extremely exciting and as there's no one better than someone who has "been there, done that", here's what ex-study abroad students had to say about their university experience abroad:

Germany

"I haven't found it very different. They start earlier. In the UK, the earliest is 9am. They start at 8am here. Lectures are the same. One major difference I would note is that here in Germany they don't have societies like UK universities do. I started horse riding at my home university. However here they don't have that opportunity. So if you have a hobby or interest, you have to find one yourself, a public one. Most of my classes that I do here are at the Sprachzentrum, which is where they have a lot of language classes for foreign students. You get homework; I wouldn't say it was too much. To learn a language though or to improve you do need to do extra work/homework outside of class." Anna Mathers, Germany

"[E]xams are at quite short notice [and it was] not clear what is expected (although this might be because I was with final year students). There was quite a lot of work, but it really depends on your understanding of the language. I found that as my knowledge of the language grew, I didn't need to spend so long on things (which was good, as the workload increased through the semester)." E. Johnson, Germany

"Not [very] different in the approach however at the end of the classes the students would bang on the tables to applaud the lectures." Jordan Wallace, Germany

Canada

"Education system was really different in Canada, compared to the UK. Firstly, they assist you a lot by giving you lots of small and frequent homework, which all count towards your final year mark. I remember being overwhelmed at how much work you get from day 1 (although they were all small amounts at a time) for each class. For example, for one class, I had weekly homework and also weekly 'quizzes', which is like a mini test. These were really easy to get good marks in and also pace you. On top of this, I had 'midterms' which is like a mini exam. The number of midterms you have for a class and the timing all depends on the nature of the work covered in class and professor. For one class, I had one midterm, right in middle of the term (as the name suggests) and for another, I had 3 midterms, all spread out even across the term. My university in

England has 3 terms which are about 8-10 weeks long, but at UBC, they have 3 semesters (out of which you will only take 2), each running for 14 weeks long. They had 'finals' (main exams) which were at the very end of each semester. The weightings of the exams totally depend on the course. It may only be 40% of your final mark if you had lots of midterms, or it may be 80% if you only had 1 midterm throughout the semester. Compared to the UK, I found that there wasn't too much independence given to you in terms of how you work, but I thought all the professors were really good at assisting and wanted to make sure all the students were satisfied with the help they were receiving. What I found most happy about was how enthusiastic all the professors were as well, compared to the professors at my university. They were able to really show how passionate they were about their subject which was both encouraging and motivating for me. Overall, I was more than satisfied with the quality of education I received, despite the lack of independence there was." Y. Arai

USA

"For my subject (Politics) and other Humanities (as I'm told by friends) the workload is very different. Much more regular assessment in the form of quizzes, group exercises, midterms as well as finals, papers. Be prepared to be doing a fair bit of work for each topic. It's not overly difficult, and I'd say they are looking to give people marks so you achieve quite highly. Also look for easy chances for extra credit, it's free marks. Classes are much smaller, and change between being lectured by the teacher to having interactive discussions in the class. Teaching style varies significantly between teachers, as does the breakdown of where marks come from, so be attentive to the syllabus." A. Potter, USA

"It is completely different to the UK system, with smaller classes and closer relationships with professors. Classes are more interactive and professors tend to lecture less, focusing more on in class and group discussions. For final or midterm exams they made you aware or hinted at what the questions would be so we had a focus for our revision. I thought it was also good that they have continuous exams and in class tests because then there was less to learn and less pressure for the final exam. I feel that professor's mark less harsh too therefore it was much easier to get good grades. I felt the workload was a lot less compared to in the UK and I rarely felt under pressure or stressed from deadlines. The regular assignments I usually had to write were no longer than 1500 words and I found it a lot easier to keep on top of work." Becky Chantry, USA

"The fact that theirs is four years was the first thing, which meant I was taking 3rd year classes as a 2nd year so felt challenged. Plus, most of the classes were older than me. But it helps knowing that you are competent at that level – my home university would not have made me do 3rd year classes otherwise. Also, the whole general education classes in first year seem like a good idea, and leaning other things throughout your time at university does too. However, the amount of grumbling I got about it makes me wonder if it's a good thing British degrees are subject focused. Compared to home, there was much more work. Every week I had to study for mini-tests, post 400 word discussions on BlackBoard, hand in essays, present to the class on a reading – the list could go on. But it's good, because it keeps you motivated. And if I'm honest, I think the work was not quite as tough as the UK, which made life a little easier." G. Sheen, USA

"American universities tend to give lots of little bits of work, rather than an essay that holds half of the marks. That meant I was doing a lot more work but it wasn't worth as much so I didn't feel under as much pressure. It was a little bit like doing A levels again, although I'd say there's a lot more reading that is a must. I still found time to socialise though so it wasn't a problem." M. Nichols, USA

"Best way of describing it is like being back in school. Lectures are called classes; work set is referred to as homework. Registers are commonly called in classes with marks deducted for poor attendance. The system tends to be a greater amount of work, but weighted less and much less challenging than the UK in comparison. Most assignments can be knocked out without much thought if you paid attention to stuff at your home institution. At UNC however you have ability to freely choose classes outside your degree (subject to home institution approval) which is nice to have some variety. Yes, though can vary from weekly tasks and quizzes with pop quizzes and presentations followed by a final exams to one term paper of long length and final exam. All classes have midterms which are exams in the 'middle' (not always the case – can be anything from two weeks into the semester to the week before finals) of the semester." A. Woods, USA

"The university system is a lot more like A-Levels. You are out of lectures and in class, structured like seminars, where the focus is on discussion and being involved. 3 out of the 4 classes I took had participation marks which terrified me at first but everyone loves an English accent so you can tot these us quite quickly! The system itself felt quite familiar and I don't think it's as different as you'd expect. Exams are different and lots include multiple choice, but this isn't as easy as it may seem! You are stripped back to before you did footnotes and using secondary sources but this left us exposed rather than top of the class as we are used to relying on other peoples arguments rather than forming our own. It was a lot of work, but it was never too much. You have to get used to doing the work because they will call on you as soon as they know your name. The deadlines were fair for the work counts and I liked the stream of work because you don't have a chance to become complacent." J. Higham, USA

Australia

"The system isn't that different to the UK except things are better organised. Their online system is really good. All my exams are multiple choice which is different as I am used to writing essays for exams. The amount of work is really well balanced; sometimes I think I work way too hard to achieve 5% of the overall grade however I have been informed that the system is changing next year. It will be better balanced." N. Maximchuk, Australia

France

"We had less work but we were meant to because Cardiff wanted us to have time to experience the culture. Once my marks are converted to Cardiff marks I definitely do better than I thought I was doing. Lectures were a bit of a shock at the beginning. All of my classes last two hours and only about half the teachers use PowerPoint presentations/OHPs. The level of economics was quite basic so it was just a case of getting used to the style of lecture/ getting very good at listening in French! None of my modules required seminars or homework but this varies from course to course. As a result the only extra work I

have done is optional and usually involves copying up notes."
Elisabeth Clement, France

"It was different, there was a lot more contact time, and lectures were longer, but I didn't really have any seminars or opportunities for discussion. I was allowed to submit essays instead of taking exams like the French students; this allowed me more time to draft my form of assessment – working on the quality of the French in particular. There really wasn't much preparation for classes besides reading the main text that was the subject of whatever module it was." Jennifer Ball, France

"Extremely! It was not organised or up to date. You can't enrol online; it has to be done by hand. There were mostly blackboards and a few whiteboards. The rooms were not in great condition either. Also, for some exams you had to ask at the "Scolarité" when and where they were because the teachers didn't know. That was a bit weird and I didn't realise this until it was too late and I ended up missing some exams because no one informed me. You are very much left to fend for yourself. Some teachers gave no work and others gave huge amounts. It was all down to the teacher you had. Sometimes it was too much." P. Howard, France

"In all honestly, I hated the university system in France. I found it so much more pressured, and as an international student, I feel that we didn't receive much support of the university. The English students were constantly put down by the French lecturers, and when we had an issue or concern, the lady who dealt with the admin issues would have no idea what to do! Our lectures would be 3 hours long each, and our in our seminars, we would be put on the spot, which we found really stressful. We did receive a lot of work to do, and we were constantly being tested. on top of all that, we would have 3 hours of lectures per module to go through each week which I found too much compared to the one hour in England that I would have." Sonia Devi, France

"Longer hours and longer terms. They started the 6th September and finished at the very end of June. For Maths, there was one 80 minute lecture to each 160 minute tutorial. In England we have at least two lectures to each tutorial if not three. There were very few, or no in some cases, examples in the lectures, and the tutorials were 100% examples. The two were taught by different lecturers, and at times it seemed that the material covered in the tutorials had nothing to do with the lectures. This seemed to make the courses twice as difficult to follow. The amount of classes I had each week, and the length of the tutorials seemed to make independent work outside of university a lot less necessary than in England. There was a lot of work, but there is in England too." Rachel Howle, France

Spain

"More teaching time, a little bit more like college than University at home. Most of it is more exam focused, I found that although some of the exams didn't seem too hard, the marking was quite harsh and I didn't do as well as I had hoped. A lot more people will fail subjects here than at home and have to retake. The first term I didn't have too much; mostly just week to week stuff. This term my classes have given more work, I'm sure that this amount in England would be no problem but obviously as it is all in Spanish it takes much longer as is a bit more daunting. Obviously writing an essay in English is much easier than in Spanish!" Hannah Bowditch, Spain

"Very different. They do not teach in lecture/seminar format and have a very strong and close relationship with their teachers. They gave a lot of work in the sense that it was

treated like school with regular assignments and homework."
Naila Missous, Spain

Singapore

"Very different, at least in the Faculty of Arts and Social
Sciences. The assessments and styles of learning are two key
differences. There's way more small-group tutorial-based stuff
and class participation is often assessed (which is good because
it encourages you to participate and prepare for tutorials). They
have more components to modules, and final exams are rarely
worth more than 60% of the total mark – it is usually more like
30 or 40%. So there's continuous assessment to keep you on
your toes (I prefer it). There is also a much wider choice of
modules than in Manchester: I was able to choose from about
300 modules in the faculty and electives are encouraged. On the
other hand, I feel academic standards are more rigorous in
Manchester/UK with referencing seemingly less important here
and lecturing quality slightly lower than in Manchester. They do
give quite a lot of work, but not too much; just right! I think it
might be different for engineering and sciences though as I hear
a lot of complaints from friends. Languages are also taught very
intensively (I did Malay in the first semester)." O. Reynolds,
Singapore

Sweden

"It was only slightly different in that the classes are taken one at
a time instead of all at the same time, so each class is more
intense, but it was nice to have a change. My first class was
minimal work outside of class, however my second class was
from their master's programme and so was little contact time
but more work outside of class. However I would not say it was
too much" Richard Latham, Sweden

Russia

"We studied in the Centre for International Education at Moscow State University, and I don't think it was a typical experience of the Russian university system, because it was geared towards language education for foreigners! We studied in small groups of about 6 or 7 students, and had the same teacher all the time. So in that respect it was different to studying at university in the UK, but it's not how Russian students would study. The workload was a lot less than here, as I think they wanted us to have lots of time to just enjoy being in Russia and do other things too. We'd get maybe an hour's worth an evening, but our teacher was generally pretty relaxed about making us do much! She was more up for getting us to have experiences, than learn grammar, which I appreciated!" Esther Harper, Russia

Belgium

"It was a bit different, lectures are all 2 or 4 hours here which is unusual for a law student. Participation is also expected in some of the lectures and there are no tutorials, but apart from that it is very similar. There is quite a lot of reading some of which you are supposed to do before classes in order to participate which can be a bit much." Kate Allen, Belgium

Austria

"1.5 hour lectures instead of 1 hour lectures. When the lecturer has finished talking all the students knock on the table as a kind of thank you which was weird! It's different because students do not pay tuition fees so sometimes I met people who were just trying out a few different degrees, you could be enrolled for up to 3 I believe. No, and one of my exams was actually cancelled short notice and the teacher just used our essays to give us our marks! Also the exam I did do wasn't invigilated like my exams are in Durham. Furthermore if you fail an exam there are 2 further resit dates, or alternatively you could just choose to enrol for an exam at a later date when you have more time. A combination of factors like this one made me feel that it's easier to get a degree at Vienna university than at Durham!" Jyoti Careswell, Austria

Just as all home universities are different, as you've seen above, all host universities are different too, with no two being alike. But the information above gives you a good idea of what to expect academically. Remember: don't get too bogged down in university work. You will have a lot to do and it is important to do well as in most cases a year abroad counts towards you final grade at home, but there's also a lot more to year abroad than just studying; there's a whole world of culture out there to go and see, so go and enjoy yourself.

Chapter 9: Working

So, you've sorted out your work placement and know where you're going, what next? What can you expect over the next year? In this chapter, we'll go over previous year abroad students' advice about going on a work placement in a foreign country.

Be Prepared

As with almost everything on your year abroad, one of the most important things is to be prepared and there are several things you should take into account when you're going to work abroad.

One of the first things is to make sure you're allowed to work abroad. If you're receiving an ERASMUS grant or if you have to have a visa to gain entrance to your country of choice, make sure you check your conditions to make sure that you're allowed to work. If you receive the ERASMUS grant, it's highly likely that you're not allowed to take on a part-time job too. Also, many visas, if they allow you to work, restrict the number of hours and sometimes the type of employment you can undertake.

Also, make sure you have a detailed CV or resume to take with you including photocopies and originals of any certificates or qualifications you might need. Possible employers want to see proof of what you put on a CV so make sure you have all those on you to avoid the added stress of trying to get someone from home to find them and send them out to you – causing unnecessary delays.

Finding a job before you leave is a must and for most universities it's a pre-requisite to going on your year abroad. However, some people do try and find a job once they are there and often find that they waste a lot of time researching and contacting people when they arrive. If you are planning to find a job this way, do your research before you leave.

5 things to ask your future employer

Part of being prepared for your work abroad year is researching what the company and your future job will be. Turning up with only limited information and now having contacted them is not a great way to start your year abroad and it will only lead to you being more stressed out than you need to be. It's hard to know what to ask and you might forget something important, remember it later, only to forget it again. So, here's a list of the 5 things you must ask your future employer before you leave (for their benefit and for yours!).

1. What kind of work will I be doing?

It sounds obvious but it's amazing how many people go on their year abroad placement without really knowing what they are going to be doing. Not knowing what you're going to be doing means that you can't prepare and you certainly can't get any essential vocabulary together before you turn up on your first day.

2. What can I expect from you?

Knowing what you can expect from an employer and asking them straight about it means less ambiguity for you both. This way, your expectations are relevant to the job you're going to be doing and there's less confusion around what to expect from your employer in regards to pay, holidays and free time.

3. What do you expect from me?

Again, this will help clear up a lot of ambiguity as you'll know exactly what it is that you need to do and what is expected of you. This will also be a warning sign of problems to come if the employer outlines unreasonable demands.

4. What language will I be working in?

Lots of people turn up on their year abroad placement thinking that they will be given all the work in their target language. However, more often than not, this isn't the case and they end up being given all the work in their native language. If this is something important to you, make sure your employer knows about it from the very beginning, that way, there are no surprises for either of you.

5. What's the dress code?

In your home country people might go to work in suits and ties but do they in the host company? Many places are much more relaxed these days in regards to what their employees wear to work. Ask them and get to know what you're going to need.

Real Student Experience
Turned up the first day in Paris in a tie and got laughed at, haha! Ed Millar, France and Peru

Money

Make sure you plan financially for working abroad. It's really important to ask your employer how much you will be making as this may or may not cover all of your year abroad expenses. Knowing beforehand will allow you to be able to plan what you need to have to get by.

Chapter 10: Teaching

Teaching your native language, whether to primary or high school students or even adults, is an extremely rewarding job, and it's a very exciting placement, directly due to the unpredictability of students. As I taught English myself whilst on my year abroad, across the next few pages, I'm going to give you my advice and that of other students who went on year abroad and taught.

There's a lot that goes into teaching. I mean, the kids have to learn something at the end of the day, you have to try and control and monitor their behaviour as well as liaise with the other teachers. Sometimes it can seem stressful but the rewards at the end of the day are amazing. You have the privilege of guiding someone through their studies for a whole year, seeing them flourish as you teach them how to weave together the rich tapestry of your native language and it's a truly incredible feeling when, at the end of your time in the school, one of your students comes up to you and thanks you for everything you've done. I'm not going to lie, it was an amazing feeling when some of my students came up to me at the end of a lovely concert they had done for me and said thank you. They had really enjoyed learning the language and seemed to have gotten something from it too.

You might be thinking that all that is good and well but what about the first lesson? What do you do when one of the kids is going a bit crazy? What if I don't know what to do in a lesson?

The great thing about teaching is that all these things do happen but you just adapt and move forward. The key to great teaching is to be flexible and be able to respond to what's happening in the classroom. Maybe you've prepared something and it isn't working, or the kids aren't interesting, there's no point struggling on and trying to get them interested in something they just don't want to do, but normally from that one idea, you can be flexible and change it a little bit so that it's more fun for them or so that it engages them more. So, I suppose, lesson one in how to teach your native language is be flexible and go with the flow. Don't be afraid of saying yes to ideas proposed by other members of staff and remember, if you're a language assistant, the kids are there to hear you speak and to get them speaking and learning so take every opportunity to engage with them.

Going into that first lesson is going to be a bit nerve-wrecking. You're going to wonder what's going on and not really know what to do. At the end of the day, most people who teach on their year abroad and become language assistants are not fully qualified teachers. So, don't feel like you have to be. Yes, you have to plan lessons. Yes, you have to teach the kids things about your culture and get them to speak, and, yes, you might get involved with extra-curricular activities but if you are a language assistant, you should not be responsible for disciplining and the kids should see it as something exciting to have you in the classroom. In your first lessons you're probably going to be talking a lot about yourself and about your home town. Let the kids get to know you (always maintaining certain boundaries!) and try to avoid those inevitable "Miss, do you have a boyfriend?", "Sir, do you have a girlfriend" questions with a smile and a 'that's none of your business' attitude while still being friendly. Take some souvenirs from your life at home, from your home town and from your university for the kids to have a look at and to keep their attention while they're trying to understand you. Maps and leaflets can be turned into little activities to move the lesson on and you could even do a mini-quiz about you and your home town to see who was really paying attention.

One of the many benefits of teaching is that you get to liaise with natives every day when you're at work. Although most will want to speak with you in your native language, make sure you come to a deal where you speak both languages so that you get something out of it too. There are some many opportunities and there will be people within the school who you can chat to who will only want you to speak in their language – this is such a great opportunity that you should always jump at it with both hands. It's not easy going up to someone and talking in a foreign language but the great thing about being at work is that you have a common interest: work! Take advantage of this, tell them about how great their tutor group is and spark up a conversation. This is often how you find out about places you'd never known existed. On the same note, accept every invitation offered by your work colleagues! There are always lots of opportunities to socialise and these really shouldn't be sniffed at. You never know, you might end up at Halloween parties, dinners with other teachers, Christmas parties – just say yes and see where it takes you.

> Real Student Experience
>
> *Be friendly with the teachers at school and they will almost certainly feed you and invite you to do fun things. Anon. Germany*

Planning your lessons can be tiresome and it really depends on what your school expects from you (another great reason to get in touch with them as soon as you know where you will be placed!). Some schools will expect you to teach full lessons on your own, where the class' regular teacher sits at the back and monitors behaviour. Whereas most schools will expect you to give parts of lessons, maybe a speaking exercise or to come up with a new activity and then you support the teacher, either by helping when reading out texts so that they get their pronunciation right or you might be asked to help out by taking one child out of the class at a time to speak with you one on one. There are lots of possibilities and you should check with your school as to what they expect you to do. Obviously, if they expect you to teach a full lesson, you'll need to make sure you have enough activities and learning points to get you through the lessons (and a couple of backups in case you need to change at the last minute). But if you're only expected to teach certain parts of the lessons then you need to plan appropriately. There's a list at the end of this chapter with lots of resources you can take a look at and don't forget a good search on the internet can bring up loads of ideas and lots of teaching resources (you don't have to pull them off the internet but you could use them for inspiration if you want to design your own resources).

OK, I had a great time but what about other year abroad students? The majority had a wonderful time and here's what they had to say about it:

"I had already thought about lessons before I went to Mexico and had gone on the British Council website for some plans. We were also given some ideas during the training week. My school lacked a lot of resources (I only had access to a white board) so I was very thankful that I had taken my own speakers and that I was creative! My first lesson was very nerve-racking: I was in front of 52 14-16 year olds. The teacher I was with suggested that they ask me some questions about myself and that I ask them some simple questions (all in English). They were so interested in me and some of the nicest teens I've ever met; I soon felt at ease. My first class at the British Council with the adults was equally scary but I soon found what worked and was able to have fun and make lots of friends. I really enjoyed the experience: it is priceless experience which I will take with me throughout the rest of my life. I learnt so much and am considering a career in teaching." C. Lorbiecki, Mexico

"My first day seemed very busy although looking back now I think there was just a lot to take in. Everyone was really nice to me and conscientious that I was nervous. I introduced myself to the students and they asked me a few questions which I followed up in the following lesson with a PowerPoint presentation about me. I was introduced to a lot of other teachers on my first day and I remember getting lots of kisses from everybody as I was introduced to different colleagues." L. Meaden, Spain

Teaching your native language can really be an amazing experience and, as with everything on your year abroad, it is what you make it. Being resourceful, friendly and open will get you far and you'll enjoy it immensely.

Lesson Resources

Planning a lesson can be daunting if you've never done it before but there are plenty of resources out there that can help you on your way, check out these ones to start with:

- British Council Teaching Assistant website http://www.teachingenglish.org.uk/language-assistant (there's even a Facebook page: http://www.facebook.com/TeachingEnglish.BritishCouncil)
- Sparknotes for literature based lessons http://www.sparknotes.com/
- http://iteslj.org/questions for conversation questions
- http://www.esl-galaxy.com/ for worksheets and activities

Those are just a few that were highlighted by previous year abroad students and there are plenty of free teaching resources on the internet. You might just use them to give you ideas, but they're a great place to start.

Chapter 11: Hard times

Sometimes things aren't so good on your year abroad and sometimes everything is not fine. Hardly anybody will tell you about this bit but there can be moments on your year abroad where things get a bit on top of you or you miss home more than you thought. I was really shocked both before I went on my year abroad and once I came back that nobody spoke about the bad times. It was all 'I had an amazing time!', 'Every moment was brilliant' etc. etc. and that's just not quite right. Everyone has down moments. It's true, it does vary. Some people will have a few small down moments which will probably go as quickly as they came after a day or two, whereas it can be worse for others. This can catch you totally unawares and you might be reading this thinking that it won't happen to you.

I want to be open and honest with you as that is what many ex-year abroad students mentioned was lacking when they spoke to their professors and their fellow students. They complained that everyone just say "everything is going to be fine" rather than explaining what might happen and what they could do about it. It's hard to open up about when things go bad, especially given that it can sometime seem like everyone else is having an amazing time except you.

It might not happen to you but chances are you will have a couple of down moments during your year abroad. This is no one's fault and it does happen to everyone so try and remember that you will get through it and everything will return to normal.

When you feel down on your year abroad, it is usually attributable to one of two things: culture shock and homesickness (or loneliness) (and what doesn't help is that one can feed the other).

Homesickness/Loneliness

I want to start by saying that it is totally normal to feel a bit homesick and a bit lonely on your year abroad. This is a big, amazing year and sometimes it can feel a bit scary, especially when you realise you're on your own in a foreign country, probably for the first time in your life. The only thing you need to know is that it will pass. You won't feel like that all the time and more than likely it will be a lot worse in the beginning than it will be once you've been there for a month or so.

Human beings are creatures of habit, so when we're taken out of our comfort zone, which is what happens in a big way on year abroad, we may feel scared, excited, nervous, lonely and many, many more emotions we had never felt before going on a year abroad.

The good news is that humans are great at adapting to circumstance and so are you! It takes some people longer than others but you will adapt to your new life, and, hey, you never know, you might end up liking it even more than your old one.

> Real Student Experience:
>
> *I felt very alone at the beginning and didn't want to admit it as I was under the impression everyone else was having an amazing time, when they were probably experiencing a similar thing to me. Anon. Germany*

The other great thing to know (and not many people will admit this) is that everyone is feeling the same. This might be to a greater or lesser extent, but everyone is feeling the same way.

Everyone gets a bit lonely on year abroad, everyone feels a bit homesick at times, and everyone gets through it and doesn't let it spoil this amazing experience. Talk to other year abroad students about this and get it off your chest. It's more than likely that someone will say "Wow! I'm feeling the same but I thought I was the only one".

This is a common problem when feeling a bit down when you're on year abroad – you can sometimes feel like you are the only one going through those feelings. When you're feeling sad, everyone seems like they're having a much better time than you are. If you feel like this, make the effort to talk to the people around you and you'll feel much better when you realise that you are all in this together and you will all help each other get through the hard times too.

A note on culture shock:

Culture shock can be a big thing if you're not prepared for it. No matter where you are going, whether it's a neighbouring country or one far away, the culture may be very different. The world is huge and everybody is different and that's one of the things that makes this life we have so amazing. However, those differences can come as a bit of a surprise occasionally and when you're on year abroad; you can feel at a bit of a loss when it happens.

Personally, I only experienced real culture shock once and it wasn't a very nice experience. I suppose, with only hoping across the water to Spain, I didn't really expect there to be any. But there definitely is and you should be aware of it.

If you do experience a bit of culture shock, try and recognise how you are feeling and then let go. OK, maybe this is something that you don't like or it makes you feel a bit uncomfortable, but you have to be there for a whole year so it's best to just go with the flow and if you can, avoid those kinds of situations.

Beating the Blues

So, now you know what homesickness can be like, what can you do when you experience it? Well, ex year abroad students have pointed out numerous ways that can help you get back on your feet when you're having a rubbish day.

- Good thing to do is try and Skype regularly, as well as keep yourself surround with friends to keep your mind off it. A. Potter, USA
- You just need to think to yourself 'you can do this' and 'it will be over soon'. That's mainly for the getting stuff sorted at the beginning which was definitely the hardest part for me. Elisabeth Clement, France
- I just spent more time with other people when I was feeling a bit overwhelmed, as I found that if I were alone I felt worse." E. Johnson, Germany
- You just have to realise that a year can go by so quickly, and you don't want to regret any part of it, or miss out on experiences because maybe you don't feel in the best of moods. Jennifer Ball, France
- There wasn't much anyone could say or do to make me feel better but I tried to distract myself by keeping busy and having things to look forward to. It also helped to have friends that were feeling the same way too. L. Meaden, Spain

Real Student Experiences

Year abroad and especially hard times whilst on a year abroad are really personal experiences and so I wanted to share some of the experiences that previous year abroad students have offered. They will show you the reality of hard times on your year abroad and demonstrate that no matter what happens, you will still have a great time on your year abroad and that these bad feelings can be overturned.

"I took me a long time to get used to the place and I had lots of down-days. However, I think that this exact experience is the one that I will value most. The difficult times have enriched my personality and have made me stronger." Anon, Spain

"I did experience some mild home sickness, but nothing too serious as I have travelled a fair bit myself. There were times as well that I felt a bit snowed under with work – my philosophy is to get as much work done during the day when people are busy with classes, so you can free up evening time to relax a bit. Try and break it up as well, spread the workload throughout the week. Didn't feel too much of a culture shock going from the UK to the US; through be prepared with the establishment's different attitudes on drinking." A. Potter, USA

"I didn't feel homesick until a few weeks in when my friends were all together over the summer and I would hear about them hanging out. I got past it though and once I started to make more friends I felt a bit more comfortable. It took me a whole semester however to settle in, when I stopped feeling homesick. It has been really easy to speak to my parents and friends due to the phone contract I have which allows me to make unlimited international calls.

I did have a huge culture shock because I assumed that because we speak the same language everything else would be the same. But the American way of life is totally different and a lot more laid back which I found difficult to get used to. I just kept myself busy to combat this." Becky Chantry, USA

"I will start by saying that I really have had an incredibly happy time here. However ... it is a roller coaster. It took a while to adjust to people being slightly curt and frosty, especially those who work in the public sector, and my worst experience was probably when a foreign taxi driver yelled at me for not knowing the exact address of my destination – my Austrian co-workers were very shocked by this, however, so I don't think that sort of thing happens a lot!

I only ever got slightly homesick in the run up to trips back to England. It's very difficult being away from your friends and family, especially as very few of them will have experienced what you do when you're abroad. Lots of people don't understand how intense it can be, and you can sometimes feel a bit left out. It's worth it, however, for all the new experiences." Bridget Wynne Wilson, Austria

"Although I cannot stress enough what an amazing year I had, I definitely had my down times. Apart from the culture shock (the apparent lack of organisation, the bureaucracy, the language barriers), I got very annoyed being stared and shouted at by the men in DF. I found that this did not happen as regularly in other areas of the country as it did in DF – something which I still cannot understand. I just learned to either ignore it, block it out with music, or yell one of the multitude of Mexican swear words that my friends were eager to teach me! Sexual harassment is common, unfortunately, in DF – especially on the metro. They tell you to travel in the 'Women's only' carriages but men still travel in them as this is not enforced by the authorities. I stopped travelling in these as this is where I had several hands on my backside (not just from men...). The worst experience was walking home one evening along the busy, well-lit street not two minutes from my apartment and having an opportunist stick his hand up my skirt. None of the people nearby did anything, not even when I was shouting at him and had hit him. This was a really low point.

I did experience some homesickness but I had regular contact with my family via email and telephone which helped. My parents even came over to visit me which was really lovely. I did not go home for Christmas or Easter which I think helped me not to miss home too much." C. Lorbiecki, Mexico

"I did definitely have times when I felt like I wasn't having as much fun as everyone else! It did help that I had a friend who had moved to a new city in England and was experiencing similar problems, so I knew it wasn't just a language/cultural issue. When you move somewhere new, it isn't easy to make new friends and suddenly whip up a social life out of nowhere! I joined a gym so that I had something to do in the evenings after work and this helped so I wasn't just sat feeling sorry for myself. After a while, I started socialising with people at work more and going to the cinema and for drinks. It was nice to meet more people and spend some time speaking German outside work." Natalie Blackburn, France and Germany

"Yeah, of course there are bad times. It's still life after all. There was one day when I changed rooms about a month into the first semester (as I was in air-con and was too expensive) and all my friends were out, none of them coming to help me move my stuff. I felt a little depressed and homesick then. I also spent large parts of the first semester questioning whether the friends I'd made were actually good friends or whether it just seemed that way because we were all having fun together, often finding myself alone after the first few weeks when I couldn't really be bothered to meet up with people all the time (as I am certainly an introvert). I've never been properly depressed by any means on the year abroad (unlike a lot during my teens) but there have been times when I've felt quite lonely, as the corridors in my halls are not massively sociable and I have just felt a bit out of the loop. Times like these have been in the minority, though, and I'm kind of used to spending a lot of time alone without it getting to me by now anyway. One night out or social event and it's all hunky-dory!" O. Reynolds, Singapore

"For me, the first month was hell. I cried every day because I didn't know what I was doing, I was hungry because the kitchen just had a hotplate and a sink which limits the options of what you can have for dinner, I missed my family and friends and thought it was horrible that no one on my corridor would make an effort to welcome me. I came very, very close to dropping out because I was completely miserable. Luckily I had made 2 good friends who tried to help me out and cheer me up. This did involve quite a lot of gin over the first month... I experienced home sickness quite a few times, especially in the first semester because everything was so different and very unorganised and difficult to deal with. In the second semester it wasn't until towards April that I got homesick and that was because I realised I hadn't been home in about 4 months, the longest I have ever been away. I also had friends telling me they missed me couldn't wait to see me which was very nice but at the same time very upsetting." P. Howard, France

"Despite having an overall amazing time in France, I did have quite a few rough patches along the way. When first moving to

France, the first few weeks I was home sick and wanted to come back! In these moments, you have to remind yourself of the reason why you decided to come abroad, and just remember that it won't last forever, and it will always be an experience you'll have for the rest of your life. When feeling down or depressed, use Skype to call home, or ring a friend and go out and do something to keep your mind off your homesickness. When I was there, I made a list of the top 10 reasons why I have come to France, and reasons why I should stay, and stuck it on my wall, so that when I was feeling down, I could remind myself. Also, when feeling down, go and visit your favourite place in the city, it always helps you put a smile on your face!" Sonia Devi, France

"I think I was in a good position because I had already done a gap year when I lived abroad before university, so being away from England and home wasn't a big deal. I did get homesick sometimes, and did miss England every now and again, but not too often! If Russia ever got too much, I would watch an English film, or go to a friend's flat and just hang out. One of my friends and I also organised to meet up once a week, just to keep up with each, after I'd moved out of accommodation, which was a good thing to have to look forward to each week, and to have an opportunity to spend time together and chat over things we were struggling with. A friend of mine who got really homesick, organised something fun for every weekend, so that she had something to look forward to each week (such as going to a museum, seeing a film at the cinema, a trip out of Moscow). She said that helped her stay positive if she was missing home." Esther Harper, Russia

"I'd say just get as involved as you can and you won't miss a thing. It's easy to keep in touch with people back home and when you're busy you'll have lots of good stories for them. If you miss people ask them to come over, everyone likes a holiday. You soon realise that things are not changing that much back home and when you see people during the holidays everyone is the same as when you left them. Just think of it like going away to university, it's no different." Kate Allen, Belgium

"Home sickness and culture shock is a bitch. Most people go through it and we were given plenty of advice about it, but it doesn't really help. Calling home using Skype and keeping up to date with wants going on helps, or friends at university to get the latest gossip. Talking to other exchanges helps a lot too as most people go through it around the same time (6-8 weeks in). I found taking time out by myself and plugging my iPod in or watching a film alone helped as well, just to relax." A. Woods, USA

"The only bad thing I can think of was the lack of funds available and saying good bye to some amazing friends. To combat the lack of funds I started working at a bar. Saying bye to friends isn't pleasant but I know I'll see some if not all again and it's easy to make new friends. I never experienced a problem with home sickness as a child my family moved around a lot so home is where my feet are. I had lived in Berlin from the age of 5-8 so the culture wasn't particularly new to me." Jordan Wallace, Germany

"I felt home sick in Austria but luckily it didn't last for long. The best way to combat any such feelings is to keep busy and keep being social! Try and make a few good friends who you feel you can turn to if you are missing home as they are what will make the difference! Also don't set your expectations too high: for example I felt down at one stage because I felt my German hadn't improved enough, but I know I developed in other ways and so it doesn't matter, sometimes you learn the most from a situation when it's not just plain sailing!" Jyoti Careswell, Germany and Austria

"I tend to get home sick when I am at university in England, so I knew it would be the same when I went to France. I tried to prepare myself by gradually going home less often towards the end of second year, so that I wouldn't be pining for home in the third week. I also bought my plane tickets well in advance so that I knew exactly when I would next be home, and could spend my time enjoying myself instead of worrying. The year abroad is a lot about socialising, but sometimes all I wanted was to be on my own. So when I felt down, I declined the invitations to go out, knowing that there would be another Erasmus party the next week." Rachel Howle, France

One of the most important things about getting through the hard times is to be aware that they might happen. If you don't know about them or are not expecting them to happen, then you can end up feeling even worse and not knowing what to do about it. If you aware something may happen, you can prepare for it and even avoid it all together if you know how.

The second most important thing to get through the hard times with ease and grace is to stay positive. No matter what happens make sure you remember that it is only one year and that you will be able to get through it. Stay positive through surrounding yourself with the great people you will meet on year abroad, avoiding thinking negative thoughts (negative thoughts only bring about more negativity) and talk to people to get it off your chest.

Chapter 12: Year Abroad Benefits

Your year abroad may end when you come home but the benefits and life lessons you learn while you're away will stay with you forever – not to mention all those year abroad stories you'll have to share with everyone for years to come! These are things that no one can ever take away from you and are things that are truly yours. So I asked previous year abroad students whether they had had a life changing experience and here's what they had to say:

"Completely. I grew up a lot in France and learnt a lot about cultures and science. I called down a lot and learnt to worry less about the small things. It gave me a bigger picture about what I wanted to do after university and where I wanted to me. My life is definitely better for the experience." B. Harker, France

"Most definitely. I am much more confident, I can get on with literally anybody regardless of age or nationality and am much more used to doing things independently. I now have no fear of turning up to a party where I only know one person and everybody speaks German, which would have been my idea of hell this time a year ago. I've learnt skills for the workplace and have a whole new set of friends. I really, really cannot recommend doing a Year Abroad enough, as I always say that I learnt more in my first two weeks here than I did in two years at university, although it was a great deal more challenging." Bridget Wynne Wilson, Austria

"I would say it was life changing. I feel certain now that this degree was the right one for me and I hope to use my Spanish as part of my career. It also made me strongly consider becoming an educator as I saw how important good teaching is, especially in a country like Mexico where an education can mean an escape from poverty. I feel inspired to do my part to help improve the global community." C. Lorbiecki, Mexico

"Yes – I've gained some really valuable work experience, met some amazing people, and seen some of the most interesting people and places in my life. It's made me sure i want to live abroad as well." Ed Millar, France and Peru

"It has been totally life changing! I have more confidence now and I know I can do a lot more than I thought I could. I feel more able to face challenges now. I'm probably also a lot more laid back. Going through the administrational nightmare at the beginning of the year has made me worry about other things a lot less because everything just seems easier to get through now." Elisabeth Clement

"It was definitely a life changing experience. I have no idea what in particular made it so but I think it is a mixture of the people I met and what I learnt through them, as well as getting to know a new culture/city and the new life style that goes with it. One of the best things that I found out through my year abroad is that I was able to challenge myself to new things and actually go about doing them with one simple thought, "I'm in Canada, on a year abroad, I only have a year, I only have one chance (to do most things) so why don't I just do it?" I really did challenge myself with lots of new activities and because of that experience; I am up for more of a challenge now and getting more comfortable at pushing my boundaries. Many of my best memories of my year abroad is when I did take on the challenge and pushed my boundaries and with this experience, I think I have also built up more confidence in my abilities." Y. Arai

"Most definitely. I am so much more confident, willing to take the lead if needs be or really support people who need it. Also, I was never overly keen on the thought of travelling without my parents, but a in early March I took the plunge and went over to the Netherlands to see my Dutch friend and one of the Belgians made it too – none of us thought we'd actually meet up again, but when the opportunity arises, I am fare more inclined to seize it now! However, I do also think a lot of things are done better in America than Britain but I don't air those views too much with people who didn't study abroad!" G. Sheen, USA

"I think so yes. It reignited my passion for learning French. It reconnected me with what I wanted to do with my life – in terms of dreams I had for the future. It did make me realise what I was capable of – in terms of being independent, and it had been a real effort on my part to work hard enough to be given the opportunity to study in university for my year abroad. It wasn't the easiest option and I was proud of myself for taking it. It meant I wouldn't be afraid to take more risks in the future for something I knew I wanted." Jennifer Ball, France

"I think I am a lot more independent now, having to find my way around a new town and get flights and organise travel by myself. I am more confident that I know what I'm doing and that I trust my own decisions more- I used to rely on others to make decisions but now I know I have the sensibilities to travel on Greyhound buses and wander around new cities at night, I have much more confidence in my abilities. It has also looked great on my CV as these new skills can transfer to any job (i.e. organisation, communication across cultures etc.) and has been a real talking point in all the interviews I have done as I think it makes me stand out!" M. Nichols, USA

"I definitely think it was life changing for me. As I said, it gave me a lot of confidence. It has also given a severe case of itchy feet; if I don't get to visit other places at least a few times a year something feels wrong! It has also made me appreciate all different kinds of towns and cities; not just the typically touristy ones.

The experience I gained working in Hamburg is also what landed me my current position in marketing at the University of Leeds, and I expect it will help me find opportunities in the future as well." Natalie Blackburn, France and Germany

"Yes. It made me so much more confident in who I was, probably because being in France I didn't really care what people thought of me/what I looked like as long as I was enjoying myself that was all that mattered. Me and my friends would laugh out loud and joke around in public and we didn't care if people thought we were annoying because we were actually enjoying ourselves and we weren't doing anything bad." P. Howard, France

"It was definitely life changing, in more ways than one. I've learnt so much about being self-sufficient, and independence. It will always be an experience that I can look back on and smile. It's also great to put on your CV and helps with employability, and it teaches you that there is so much more out there in the world than your small bubble that you live in back at home. I'm so glad that I took the opportunity and I'm proud that I stuck it out through the rough patches, and I'll never the regret the memories I made abroad." Sonia Devi, France

"It was life changing, in that the year developed a passion for Russia, Russians and Russian language, that wasn't part of me before! Now every time I think about the future, Russia/Russian is part of it! I also came back way more confident in myself, and having had some tough experiences which makes life in England seem really easy sometimes!" Esther Harper, Russia

"It definitely gives you a bit of a different perspective on a lot of things and makes you more confident speaking to new people and people from across the world but it's very similar to being a fresher in university I think it's just the next level of independence and really coping on your own which makes you more self-sufficient." Kate Allen, Belgium

"I have much more of a handle of what I want to do in the future and America really helped with my outlook and the ability to find my own voice." J. Higham, USA

"It was certainly unique, now it's over I feel very nostalgic looking back: I can go back and visit those places but it won't be the same as living there. You have a completely different appreciation of a culture when you live somewhere, furthermore if you study or work you have a role in that society, you are not just a tourist!" Jyoti Careswell, Germany and Austria

"I have learnt a lot about the French way of life, which will inevitably effect how I live my life. Equally I have met people from all over the world, who have helped me to expand my views. I have taken up new hobbies, including skiing and roller skating. These things might not have completely changed my life, but they have certainly enhanced it." Rachel Howle, France

You see, all the things mentioned above by the brave previous year abroad students, just goes to show that no matter where you go on your year abroad, it will have a major impact on you, affect you in a positive way and you'll learn and experience things that you may never have expected. All in all, you will learn new things, meet new people, make friends all around the world and above all, have one of the best years ever.

Inspiration

I couldn't end the book without sharing with you some of the amazing stories from the ex-year abroad students who collaborated in this book. I hope these stories inspire you as much as they did me. Here, I asked students what had been the best part of their year abroad. WARNING: this section will make you want to head out on your year abroad right now!

"When I think of my year abroad there isn't a particular moment or memory exactly, it's more the way of life I had while I was there. I lived alone and loved the independence I had. Being fully responsible for myself and the place I lived was great, and I loved walking to the market with my basket (very French!), checking out an art gallery, and maybe grabbing lunch in the sun with a friend. I loved speaking French, and listening to French, and just being surrounded by it all!" Jennifer Ball, France

"Meeting lots of new people and becoming part of a community. I love how generous and welcoming everyone I came into contact with was. If I was feeling down at any point, going into school would cheer me up." L. Meaden, Spain

"Experiencing a town that as a tourist I would never visit, I got to see unique places which gave me an insight in to what it was really like in America. I have loads of friends now that I can go and stay with which is really fun, and I loved the different university culture in terms of having more house parties and going to frat parties. I was so interested in the Greek system of sororities and fraternities that I am now writing my dissertation on it! In Champaign, the bar entry age is 19 which is unique (although you still have to be 21 to drink) and that is one reason

I chose to go there. This meant that instead of having to stay with house parties, we could actually go out to different bars which made the nightlife a lot more interesting than some of my course mates at other universities in the US." M. Nichols, USA

"All of the many, many, weekends and trips away! And even the weekends In Hamburg In fact. Coming home from a night out at 8am, going to Munich, Brussels, Prague, and so many more places!

And again when I was in France, spending most weekends at the beach and exploring the local area was such a great opportunity." Natalie Blackburn, France and Germany

"My holiday in Cairns! I went skydiving, snorkelling, scuba diving, crocodile touring and waterfall jumping." N. Maximchuk, Australia

"Difficult to say. It would have to be one of the trips: Sumatra was the best, although Bali/Java, Thailand and Burma were also highly epic. In Singapore, I've recently come to really appreciate and value having a group of really good friends away from 'normal life', many of whom I will definitely see again and feel some could be friends for life. Also getting laid in the first weeks was nice." O. Reynolds, Singapore

"It is actually difficult to say. I think whenever I went travelling to a new place I was really happy. It was nice to be able to get out my room and out of the local area and be able to walk around in a completely new scene. My trip to Italy was fantastic if not a little stressful at times due to a mild lack of organisation and almost missing the flight there. Travelling, though, was what made it all worthwhile, even just the day trips to a different town an hour away." P. Howard

"Meeting new people and the Kiruna trip as it fulfilled a lifelong dream to see the northern lights" Richard Latham, Sweden

"It's so hard to have just one best bit! I got the chance to visit Italy, and Marseille whilst I was in Paris. It was so fun, getting to see all the beautiful buildings and different cultures, and getting to swim in the sea was pretty amazing too! One of my friends visited whilst I was there, and we hired bikes out and went cycling across Paris, it was so beautiful, especially when cycling near the Eiffel tower at night." Sonia Devi, France

"Definitely living with my flatmate – we're still really close, and she's brilliant! The travelling I did was absolutely brilliant! The few weeks with the charity was great for lots of reasons, including getting to know Russian society on a new level, which was quite emotional at times but necessary if you really want to understand Russian culture, and different social groups." Esther Harper, Russia

"The best bit I think is the freedom, to meet new people and travel. In Belgium students go home every weekend and this inspires us to travel and explore. All the different people give you different insights into what you're seeing and a different perspective to look at." Kate Allen, Belgium

"At the moment: going to Cancun, Mexico for Spring Break. But I haven't started my epic summer road trip yet!" A. Woods, USA

"The chance to go travelling was mega and something I was really excited for. I also really enjoyed the atmosphere of the university; though it was on campus and I am so used to the city and Manchester, the 'team spirit' was huge, and everyone was more than friendly in class. It really encourage me to speak out and get involved in lessons, meaning I have come back with a whole new wave of confidence and outlook on life." J. Higham, USA

"Making friends with so many different people. Eating different foods and the parties" Jordan Wallace, Germany

"The independence: making it my own unique experience, different from everybody else! When my Dad came out to visit me I realised how I had established a whole life for myself completely on my own, and I could even give him a complete Vienna tour, you don't realise how well you know a city until you have to show someone else around.

I loved the freedom when it came to travelling: in Europe you can be more spontaneous, hop on a train last minute and don't have to book flights way in advance." Jyoti Careswell, Germany and Austria

"The people I met made my year abroad. Both international and local people helped me have an amazing time discovering and exploring Bordeaux and the surrounding area." Rachel Howle, France

So… what will your best year abroad moment?

A Letter from Nicola

Wow, I can't believe we're at the end of the book already! I just wanted to take this last opportunity to say that I hope you really enjoyed reading this book and that you've now got the confidence to go abroad and have a really great time.

I would really like to thank all of the amazing contributors who gave so much to this book through participating in interviews and surveys. It would not have been possible without them and I am truly grateful for all their help and support.

From preparing to leave to how to get the most out of your year abroad, I've tried to cover everything that came up in the interviews, but if you've got any further questions, why not ask me and other year abroad students on our Facebook and Twitter pages or email me at Nicola@survivingyouryearabroad.com, I'm sure we can get an answer for you.

Have a wonderful time and I would love to hear how much you enjoyed your year abroad so don't be a stranger and let us know what breath-taking sights you saw and how much you enjoyed it! You never know, you might appear in the next book!

Your year abroad is what you make it, so why not make it amazing!

Bon voyage!

Nicola

Get involved

Do you want to pass on your year abroad experience to future year abroad students and help them overcome the worries you have now? Well, there are loads of ways you could pass on your knowledge. You could take part in a quick interview about your year abroad, you might choose to fill in our expenses sheet to pass on your budgeting problems or maybe you fancy speaking to future year abroad students about your experiences? Or even better, maybe you fancy getting involved in many different aspects?

Whatever takes your fancy, we've made it really easy for you to get involved and pass your legacy on! It's really simple to get involved, just send an email to getinvolved@survivingyouryearabroad.com to find out you can help out.

Disclaimer: Any comments and quotes made by ex-year abroad students do not necessarily represent the views and opinions of Surviving Your Year Abroad or any of its affiliates of partners.

This eBook is © copyrighted by Surviving Your Year Abroad. The eBook and its contents may not be reproduced or used in any way, in whole or in part, in any format, without prior permission from Surviving Your Year Abroad.

About the Author

In 2009, Nicola went on her own year abroad and had a great time. But before she left she felt apprehensive. Turning up in a little Spanish town with little to no information about what to do can be quite scary!

Thinking she was the "only one" with these worries, she didn't mention them and just got on with it as most students seem to do.

She had an amazing year abroad flitting around Spain but the part she was most surprised about was when she returned home: everyone was talking about how ill prepared they felt about their year abroad! Everyone has been nervous before leaving and no one has known what to expect. Of course, we had all the advice from the university but that can only go so far due to time constraints. Seeing all these students talking about their experiences, and then thinking about the students who were about to embark on this amazing year brought about this project.

After juggling her business, two cats, and living in a foreign country, the project finally came back to life. Nine months of hard work later and the result is what you see here: lots of real information about what your year abroad is really going to be like.

Her mission is simple: make sure that you have the best time on your year abroad.

Feel free to get in touch with her by emailing her at Nicola@survivingyouryearabroad.com

Thank you

I just want to say a really heartfelt thank you to all of the previous year abroad students who took part in the surveys and interviews that went into this project. This really wouldn't have been half as exciting or interesting without you guys to help me out.

So thank you to:

Elizabeth Lewis

Ed Millar

Hannah Bowditch

Jordan Wallace

E. Johnson

Jyoti Careswell

Y. Arai

B. Harker

Ric Latham

Naila Missous

Anna Mathers

M. Nichols

L. Meaden

A. Potter

Rachel Howle

Elisabeth Clement

S. Eastaff

P. Howard

Sonia Devi

Kate Allen

G. Sheen

A. Woods

J. Higham

Bridget Wilson

O. Reynolds

Natalie Blackburn

Esther Harper

C. Lorbiecki

Jennifer Ball

and

Becky Chantry

31985562R00063

Printed in Great Britain
by Amazon